HOW TO READ

Available now

How to Read Darwin by Mark Ridley
How to Read Freud by Josh Cohen
How to Read Hitler by Neil Gregor
How to Read Nietzsche by Keith Ansell Pearson
How to Read Sade by John Phillips
How to Read Wittgenstein by Ray Monk

Published Autumn 2005

How to Read Foucault by Ian Hacking
How to Read Heidegger by Mark Wrathall
How to Read Jung by Andrew Samuels
How to Read Marx by Peter Osborne
How to Read Shakespeare by Nicholas Royle

Forthcoming

How to Read de Beauvoir by Stella Sandford
How to Read Derrida by Penelope Deutscher
How to Read Sartre by Robert Bernasconi

HOW
TO
READ

NIETZSCHE

KEITH ANSELL PEARSON

Granta Books
London

Granta Publications, 2/3 Hanover Yard, Noel Road, London N1 8BE

First published in Great Britain by Granta Books 2005

A CIP catalogue record for this book
is available from the British Library.

3 5 7 9 10 8 6 4 2

Typeset by M Rules

Printed and bound in Great Britain by
Bookmarque Limited, Croydon, Surrey

For Nicky — with deep love

CONTENTS

Acknowledgements   viii
Series Editor's Foreword   xi
Introduction   1

1 The Horror of Existence   7

2 Human, All Too Human – Historical versus
      Metaphysical Philosophy   18

3 Nietzsche's Cheerfulness   30

4 On Truth and Knowledge   41

5 On Memory and Forgetting   52

6 Life is a Woman, or the Ultimate Beauties   61

7 The Heaviest Weight   72

8 The Superman   82

9 Nihilism and the Will to Nothingness   94

10 Behold the Man   105

Notes   117
Appendix   119
Chronology   121
Suggestions for Further Reading   124
Index   128

ACKNOWLEDGEMENTS

I am grateful to Simon Critchley for inviting me to write this book for the 'How to Read' series, and to Duncan Large for allowing me to amend his now standard Chronology of Nietzsche. George Miller and Bella Shand of Granta Books have contributed in invaluable ways to the maturation of this book, and I wish to express my gratitude to both of them. Special thanks to Michael Bell, my colleague at Warwick, for his insights into the topic of 'redemption' that I have put to work in chapter eight.

For permission to publish copyright material in this book grateful acknowledgement is made to the following publishers:

Cambridge University Press: for the selections from *The Birth of Tragedy & Other Writings*, trans. Ronald Speirs (1999); *The Gay Science*, translated Josefine Nauckhoff (2001); *Human, All Too Human: A Book for Free Spirits* (two volumes), translated by R. J. Hollingdale (1986); and *On the Genealogy of Morality*, translated by Carol Diethe (1994).

Penguin: for the selections from *Thus Spoke Zarathustra: A Book for Everyone and No One*, translated by R. J. Hollingdale (1961); and *Ecce Homo*, translated by R. J. Hollingdale (1992). References given throughout the text are to aphorism and section numbers, not page numbers.

The universe must be splintered apart; respect for the universe unlearned; what we have given the unknown and the whole must be taken back and given to the closest, what's ours. Kant said: 'Two things remain forever worthy of admiration and awe' [the starry heavens above and the moral law within] – today we would rather say: 'Digestion is more venerable'. The universe would always bring with it the old problems, 'How is evil possible?', etc. Thus: *there is no universe*.

Nietzsche, 1886–7

To explore the whole sphere of the modern soul, to have sat in its every nook – my ambition, my torture, and my happiness.

Nietzsche, 1887

SERIES EDITOR'S FOREWORD

How am I to read *How to Read*?

This series is based on a very simple, but novel idea. Most beginners' guides to great thinkers and writers offer either potted biographies or condensed summaries of their major works, or perhaps even both. *How to Read*, by contrast, brings the reader face to face with the writing itself in the company of an expert guide. Its starting point is that in order to get close to what a writer is all about, you have to get close to the words they actually use and be shown how to read those words.

Every book in the series is in a way a masterclass in reading. Each author has selected ten or so short extracts from a writer's work and looks at them in detail as a way of revealing their central ideas and thereby opening doors onto a whole world of thought. Sometimes these extracts are arranged chronologically to give a sense of a thinker's development over time, sometimes not. The books are not merely compilations of a thinker's most famous passages, their 'greatest hits', but rather they offer a series of clues or keys that will enable readers to go on and make discoveries of their own. In addition to the texts and readings, each book provides a short biographical chronology and suggestions for further reading, internet resources, and so on. The books in the *How to Read* don't claim to tell you all you need to know about Freud, Nietzsche and Darwin, or indeed Shakespeare and the Marquis de Sade, but they do offer the best starting point for further exploration.

Rather than the available second-hand versions of the minds that have shaped our intellectual, cultural, religious, political and scientific landscape, *How to Read* offers a refreshing set of first-hand encounters with those minds. Our hope is that these books will, by turns, instruct, intrigue, embolden, encourage and delight.

Simon Critchley
New School for Social Research, New York

INTRODUCTION

Since his death in 1900 Nietzsche has received an enormous amount of attention, and controversy has always surrounded his work. Why should we continue to read him today? I think there are two main reasons. The first is that Nietzsche is the author of some of the most beautifully crafted texts to be found in the history of philosophy and remains an inspiring example of a genuinely independent philosophical spirit; his writing never fails to provoke us into thinking in ways that are challenging and often elevating. The second is that Nietzsche remains one of the greatest philosophical educators of the modern period. He exposes in a highly instructive manner the fundamental predicaments – and some of the pitfalls – of modern philosophical reasoning to which his thinking remains bound.

One is drawn to a philosopher not because one necessarily agrees with every point he makes. In my case the negotiation with Nietzsche, which has been ongoing for over two decades, has involved a constant battling with his ideas. I don't know of any serious commentator who has not had a critical relation to Nietzsche and not found aspects of his thinking troubling and problematic. The case of the post-war translator and commentator of Nietzsche Walter Kaufmann (1921–80) offers a good example. Kaufmann devoted many years of his life to translating Nietzsche, to correcting the image of him fostered by Nazism, and to introducing him to the English-speaking world. His work inspired a whole generation of scholars, especially those working in North America. But he was not a Nietzschean. Indeed, it is not clear what it would mean to be a Nietzschean. One of the pre-eminent intellectual figures of the post-war period, Michel Foucault (1926–84), contested the idea that there is such a thing as a single or core Nietzscheanism (a view endorsed by the late British philosopher Bernard Williams). Foucault suggested that the right question to ask is 'What serious use can Nietzsche be put to?' However, whilst it is the case that there is no single Nietzscheanism, Nietzsche did bequeath to us moderns a set of novel philosophical tasks, such as practising 'the gay science' and cultivating philosophical 'cheerfulness', getting to grips with the problem of nihilism and conceiving in new ways the art and science of living well (the task of the superman). Seeking to comprehend these tasks and secure the measure of them is, I believe, the best way to introduce Nietzsche to the new reader. This is what I have sought to do in this short guide.

Nietzsche was trained in philology, the study of language in its historical and comparative aspects (*philologia*, the love of learning and the love of words). As a professor of classical philology he specialised in the study of ancient Greek literary and philosophical texts. Although he often criticised the discipline for its scholasticism and pedantry, the importance it places on the arts of reading and interpretation deeply informed his work. He repeatedly stresses the value of knowing how to read well. Style for him consists in discovering the means of expression through which every state of mind can be conveyed to the reader. He presents himself in untimely or unfashionable terms as a friend of slowness (*lento*), the teacher of slow reading. The contemporary age is an age of quickness; it no longer values slowness but seeks to hurry everything. Philology can be viewed as a venerable art which demands that its practitioners take time so as to become still and slow. More than anything it is an art that teaches one how to read well, which consists in reading slowly and deeply, and with the aid of which one looks and sees in a certain and specific manner: cautiously, observantly, 'with doors left open' and 'with delicate eyes and fingers'. Nietzsche believes that reading should be an art, for which rumination is required. He stresses that an aphorism has not been deciphered just because it has been read out; rather, an art of interpretation or exegesis needs to come into play. In this guide I have sought to pay close attention to Nietzsche's words, and this has informed my explication of his ideas. In the case of a philosopher who requests that his readers learn to read him well the value of close reading cannot be underestimated.

Nietzsche wrote in a variety of styles, including the short maxim and the extended aphorism, the essay form, and the dithyramb (a passionate or inflated poem). He does not employ the aphorism for one end or purpose and many different kinds of aphorism can be found in his writings, ranging from the single sentence to an extended reflection, including a small essay, on one point. The aphorism does not have a single *raison d'être*. The word itself is first encountered in the collection of treatises *Corpus Hippocraticum* named after the physician of the fifth century BC, Hippocrates, which contained rules for good living and good health. Something of the original usage of the form undoubtedly persists in Nietzsche's writing and informs his conception of philosophical practice (he once described himself as a physician of culture). What the anecdote is to life the aphorism is to thought, something to learn how to incorporate. The aphorism serves to test the bounds of sense by making strange our encounter with things we take to be known and familiar. The word comes in fact from the Greek for definition (*aphorismos*), which contains within it the word for horizon (*horos*), and a negotiation with boundaries and horizons plays an important role in Nietzsche's thinking. In making a selection of aphorisms and sections for the purposes of this guide, my aim has been to give the reader a sense of the fundamental philosophical problems that concerned Nietzsche.

It is customary to divide Nietzsche's writings into three distinct periods: early (1872–6), middle (1878–82 and 1883–5), and late (1885–8). The first period begins with the publication of *The Birth of Tragedy* in 1872 and includes four 'untimely meditations' written in 1873–5 (on cultural philistinism, on the uses and disadvantages of history for life, on Schopenhauer as educator, and on Wagner in Bayreuth). Here Nietzsche's tasks are centred on an 'artist's metaphysics' and the need for cultural regeneration and renewal. The second period includes the 'free-spirit trilogy', comprising *Human*, *All Too Human* (two volumes), *Daybreak*, and *The Gay Science*. Here Nietzsche's tasks are centred on overcoming metaphysics and gaining a new philosophical maturity. *Thus Spoke Zarathustra* was published in 1883-5 and serves to bridge the middle and late periods. It is in this text that Nietzsche announces that the superman or overman will now be the meaning of the earth. The late period includes a number of classic texts, such as *Beyond Good and Evil*, *On the Genealogy of Morality*, *Twilight of the Idols*, *The Anti-Christ*, and *Ecce Homo*. In contrast to the 'yea-saying' task that marks the free-spirit trilogy, this set of texts is devoted to what Nietzsche called his 'nay-saying' task, involving a revaluation of all values and a fatal reckoning with Christian morality. It is in these texts that we encounter the most fantastical and problematic aspects of his thinking. The nature of this development will become clearer as the book unfolds.

In this guide I introduce the reader to essential features of Nietzsche's thinking in each one of the three main periods that characterize his intellectual development. I have not been able to do this, however, in equal measure. There are many demands that a writer has to try to satisfy with a guide of this kind, and what can be accomplished in it is extremely limited. The reader wants to know something about Nietzsche's major ideas, some details of his life, insight into his intellectual development, and so on. The writer wants to do justice to the complex character of a thinker's ideas and to present them in a way that aims to both instruct and challenge the reader. In the ten chapters that make up this guide I have sought to meet the needs of the reader, whilst at the same time remaining faithful to the questions and problems that inform my own contributions to philosophy, which have been heavily influenced by Nietzsche's ideas.

The first two chapters provide insight into Nietzsche's philosophical beginning and subsequent development. Chapter three covers the fundamental theme of the death of God and provides insight into the character of Nietzsche's philosophical cheerfulness. Chapter four looks at how Nietzsche seeks to pose some novel questions concerning truth and knowledge. Chapter five deals with the way memory and forgetting are treated in his writings. Chapters six and seven offer close readings of two aphorisms from book four of *The Gay Science*, one much more well-known and widely discussed than the other. The first is his highly enigmatic treatment of 'Vita femina'; the second is on the strange thought of eternal return. Chapter eight concerns the concept of the superman in his book *Thus Spoke Zarathustra*. Chapter nine is on his treatment of the will to nothingness and the problem of European nihilism. The final chapter looks at Nietzsche's last text, *Ecce Homo*, where I focus on his complex legacy as a philosopher.

Nietzsche does not think philosophy exists to make us better human beings – but it can make us more profound ones. He begins his great text of 1887 on the genealogy of morals on a paradoxical note, claiming that 'we knowers' – as we moderns like to think of ourselves – are essentially unknown to ourselves. To find ourselves supposes we know how to search for ourselves. He notes that we are deaf to the sounds we hear around us, including the sounds and echoes of our own being. We find it difficult to find the time needed to digest life's experiences – our heart (and our ear) is simply not in it. We exist in an absent-minded manner and are like someone sunk deep in their own thoughts who, upon hearing the twelve strokes of midday, wakes up with a start and wonders, 'what hour has just struck?' Only afterwards, upon the delay of time, do we rub our ears and ask, astonished and taken aback, 'just what did we experience then?' and 'who am I in fact?' Of necessity we are strangers to ourselves. We essentially seek to bring knowledge back home – that is, to a familiar time and place. Our desire is to see ourselves reflected always in all our events and actions. We want knowledge that is familiar and that will not place the demands of time on us. Nietzsche asks whether we are serious enough about acquiring self-knowledge and whether we can find 'enough time' for the task. In a fundamental sense this is also what is involved in learning how to read Nietzsche – to find the time to read him and to ensure that we read him 'well'.

1

THE HORROR OF EXISTENCE

Dionysiac art, too, wants to convince us of the eternal lust and delight of existence; but we are to seek this delight, not in appearances but behind them. We are to recognize that everything which comes into being must be prepared for painful destruction; we are forced to gaze into the terrors of individual existence – and yet we are not to freeze in horror: its metaphysical solace tears us momentarily out of the turmoil of changing figures.

For brief moments we are truly the primordial being itself and we feel its unbounded greed and lust for being; the struggle, the agony, the destruction of appearances, all of this now seems to us to be necessary, given the uncountable excess of forms of existence thrusting and pushing themselves into life, given the exuberant fertility of the world-Will; we are pierced by the furious sting of these pains at the very moment when, as it were, we become one with the immeasurable, primordial delight in existence and receive an intimation, in Dionysiac ecstasy, that this delight is indestructible and eternal. Despite fear and pity, we are happily alive, not as individuals, but as the *one* living being, with whose procreative lust we have become one.

Extract from *The Birth of Tragedy Out of the Spirit of Music*, section 17

Nietzsche had a number of philosophical beginnings. As a youth in the early 1860s he came into contact with a volume of essays by the American writer Ralph Waldo Emerson (1803–82), and he wrote his first philosophical essays on fate and history under its inspiration. He continued to draw inspiration from his reading of Emerson into his so-called middle period (1878–82). In our own time the American philosopher Stanley Cavell (1926–) has made an important contribution to an Emersonian appreciation of Nietzsche, focusing on the tasks of a moral perfectionism, such as the cultivation of a higher and deeper self. In the mid-1860s Nietzsche discovered Schopenhauer (1788–1860) and found that he suited his melancholic temperament. Schopenhauer had a precocious talent and was only twenty-six when he began to compose his *magnum opus*, *The World as Will and Representation* (published in 1819). Nietzsche was also greatly impressed by Friedrich Lange's magisterial *History of Materialism*, which he read on its publication in 1866. He found it a valuable aid in securing a grasp on many philosophical problems. He was also reading Goethe's (1749–1832) writings on nature and working through Kant's (1724–1804) attempt to articulate a new approach to the philosophy of art and the philosophy of nature in his *Critique of Judgement* (1790), as well as many books in the field of the natural sciences. In 1868 he wrote a perspicacious criticism of Schopenhauer's system but interestingly the critical points he makes of it – that the will in Schopenhauer's formulation of the will to life is a clumsily coined and all-too encompassing word, that it is articulated in terms of a poetic intuition and that the logical proofs offered in support of the theory fail to convince – do not figure in *The Birth of Tragedy*.

In early 1869, at the age of twenty-five, Nietzsche, who had recently begun to feel disaffected with his chosen subject of study, was appointed to Basel University in Switzerland as Extraordinary Professor of Classical Philology. He was to make an unsuccessful bid for the Chair of Philosophy a few years later. He made his first visit to Richard Wagner and his wife, Cosima, in April of that year, and in May gave his inaugural lecture on 'Homer's Personality'. In 1870 and 1871 Nietzsche lectured on topics that would form the basis of his first book, such as Socrates and tragedy and the Dionysian world-view. He felt he was about to give birth to a 'centaur', with art, philosophy and scholarship all growing together inside him. Nietzsche served as a medic in the Franco-Prussian War. On return to Basel he began to suffer from insomnia and endured serious bouts of ill-health and migraine attacks throughout the rest of his life.

Nietzsche published *The Birth of Tragedy* in the first month of 1872 with a dedication to Wagner. It shows that he was not destined to be a mere scholar or an academic philosopher. He would not let his training in classical philology restrain his ambitions for cultural renewal and he would not let his academic standing compromise his intellectual project. The book contains a highly original treatment of Greek tragedy, it makes a novel contribution to aesthetics with its exploration of the duality of the two Greek deities Dionysus and Apollo, and it stages a critical and clinical encounter with Socrates' theoretical optimism which holds that not only can the world be known but it can also be corrected (in pitting rationality against instinct Socrates is recognised as a decadent). It also represents Nietzsche's first presentation of nihilism, which in its earliest articulation is an existential affair arising from a cosmic problem, in contrast to his later stress on nihilism as a historical and cultural problem of values where mankind's highest values reach a point of devaluation. In *The Birth of Tragedy* existential nihilism manifests itself in the words of the satyr and companion of Dionysus, Silenus, who addresses us as a wretched and ephemeral species, as children of chance and tribulation in words it would be best for us not to hear: 'The very best thing is utterly beyond your reach: not to have been born, not to *be*, to be *nothing*. However, the second best thing for you is: to die soon.'

In a self-criticism of the book penned in 1886 Nietzsche said that in it he was using formulas from Kant and Schopenhauer – notably their division of the world into the two dimensions of appearance and the thing-in-itself (the unknowable 'x' behind appearance), which in Schopenhauer is the blind, impersonal and nonhuman will to life – to express ideas that had nothing to do with their systems. In this chapter I want to give a sense of what these ideas are. In *The Birth of Tragedy* Nietzsche proposes that it is only as an aesthetic phenomenon that existence and the world can be justified. Aristotle said that philosophy begins in wonder – wonder at the fact that things are how they are. For Nietzsche, by contrast, philosophy begins with horror – existence is something both horrible and absurd. It is this Nietzsche that exerted such an influence on existentialist currents of thought in the twentieth century, including the writings of Albert Camus (1913–60). Why this horror? And what role does art play in relation to it? Before we can answer these questions, it is necessary to say something about the key ideas at work in the book.

The Birth of Tragedy opens with Nietzsche defining two competing but also complementary impulses in Greek culture, the Apollonian and the Dionysian. The first takes its name from Apollo, the god of light, dream and prophecy, the shining one, while the second takes its name from Dionysos, the god of intoxication and rapture. While Apollo is associated with visible form, comprehensible knowledge and moderation, Dionysus is linked with formless flux, mystical intuition and excess. Furthermore, while the Apollonian names a world of distinct individuals, the Dionysian world names one where these separate individual identities have been dissolved and human beings find themselves reconciled with the elemental forces and energies of nature. Through Dionysian rapture we become part of a single, living being with whose joy in eternal creation we are fused.

In artistic terms, Apollo is the god of the plastic or representational arts (painting and sculpture), with a strong association with architecture, and Dionysus is the god of the non-representational art of music which is without physical form. One of the innovative aspects of Nietzsche's argument in the book is the way it contests the idealised image of the Greeks that had been handed down, depicting Greek culture as one of serenity and calm grandeur. Nietzsche's claim is that the Apollonian surface of Greek art and culture is the product of long and complex wrestling with the tragic insights afforded by the Dionysian state. Attic tragedy of the fifth century BC, contained in the work of tragedians such as Aeschylus and Sophocles, rested on a fusion of the Apollonian and the Dionysian. Nietzsche's book is a search for an adequate knowledge of the union between the two artistic powers (a union he calls a 'mystery') and of the origin of Greek tragedy.

Among other things, the search leads him to an examination of the main tendencies of Greek poetry (Homer, Archilochus and Pindar) and of the tragic chorus. Here Nietzsche accepts the prevailing Aristotelian view that tragedy has its origins in the chorus and he also accepts the argument (found in the work of Friedrich Schiller, for example) that the chorus serves as a barrier between the real, empirical world and the tragic action taking place on stage. But he dissents markedly from the view that the chorus is a representation of the spectators on stage; rather, Nietzsche sees it as representative of the Dionysian state and its insight that life remains indestructible and pleasurable in the face of the suffering and anguish that characterise our individual existence. We suffer as individuals for various reasons. Once we recognise our cosmic insignificance we know that there is no ultimate purpose to human existence; the fact of death brings this home to each individual clearly and forcefully. Life is characterised by desire (growth and procreation) and energy (its accumulation and discharge), but we know that this activity of life is not in any way centred on us.

For Nietzsche the only subject-matter of early Greek tragedy is the sufferings of the god Dionysos. He contends that right down to Euripedes, Dionysos did not cease to be the tragic hero, so that all the well-known figures of the Greek stage, such as Prometheus and Oedipus, are but masks of the original hero. It is important that we appreciate just how the god Dionysos appears on stage. His appearance as one who resembles an erring, striving and suffering individual is due to the effect of Apollo, the interpreter of dreams and the realm of appearance. In truth, however, Nietzsche says, the hero is the suffering Dionysos of the Mysteries, that is, the god who experiences the sufferings of individuation in his own person, the one who was torn to pieces as a boy by the Titans but who is also torn to pieces in the very heart of his terrible condition. He suffers because he is individuated and it is individuation that is the source and primal cause of all suffering and that needs rejecting, Nietzsche adds.

This gives us a profound and pessimistic way of looking at the world: what exists is a unity and primordial oneness; individuation is merely appearance and is the primal source of all evil; art offers the joyous hope that the spell of individuation can be broken and the unity restored. We suffer from life because we are individuals alienated from nature and because our consciousness of this separation afflicts us.

Nietzsche presents Dionysos as a Christ-like figure, and indeed throughout the text he uses theological concepts such as redemption. However, Nietzsche is presenting in *The Birth of Tragedy* a very different theodicy to the Christian one; the aesthetic justification of the world refers to the need of the primal ground itself and has little to do with us. The Greeks knew and felt the terror and absurdity of existence and created the gods Dionysus and Apollo from their most powerful needs. They were able to reach the only satisfactory theodicy there has ever been because 'do the gods justify the life of man! They themselves live it'. For Nietzsche there is nothing in their experience that suggests asceticism, spirituality or duty: 'we hear nothing but the accents of an exuberant, triumphant life in which all things, whether good or evil, are deified'.

For Nietzsche the world is a tragic play of opposites, it knows no redemption and it requires no salvation. As one commentator has noted, Nietzsche exaggerates psychological concepts to cosmic dimensions.[1] Philosophy is a matter of tragic wisdom which can be cultivated only on the basis of an insight into the primordial strife between darkness (Dionysos) and light (Apollo) – that is, between the all-devouring, formless and abysmal ground of life and the domain of light that forms individuals. A philosophy of tragic insight is one that grasps this eternal discord between the primordial oneness and individuation. This does not lead Nietzsche to embrace a passive pessimism as did Schopenhauer; in spite of the changes of appearances life proves itself to be something indestructibly powerful and pleasurable. Only art can be equal to the insight found in a philosophy of the tragic. The ancient Hellene was a human being susceptible to the deepest suffering, having seen clearly into the terrible destructions of world history and the cruelty of nature, and in danger of longing for a negation of the will akin to that of the Buddhist. However, art saves him and through art life. On account of his attempt to transpose the Dionysian into a philosophical pathos, Nietzsche would later lay claim to being the first tragic philosopher. For him the category of the tragic denotes not the purification of a dangerous emotion, such as pity or terror, through its forceful discharge, as in Aristotle's theory of catharsis; rather, it is an experience beyond pity and terror, an affirmation of the eternal joy of universal becoming, which also includes joy in destruction.

Schopenhauer borrowed the expression 'principle of individuation' (*principium individuationis*) from scholastic thinking and used it to denote the phenomenal world of time and space as that which gives us a plurality of coexistent and successive things. By contrast, the will is the thing-in-itself and outside the order of time and space. The will also lies outside the province of the principle of sufficient reason (the principle that serves to explain what something is at a specific time and place and the causal laws it is subject to), and can, therefore, be said to be groundless and primordially one (not simply one as either an object or a concept). In their coming to be and perishing away individuals exist only as phenomena of the will, which is conceived as a blind, irresistible urge. Although Nietzsche's argument in *The Birth of Tragedy* relies heavily on the terms of Schopenhauer's metaphysics, it does not simply replicate them. Apollo is conceived as the transfiguring genius of the *principium individuationis* through which redemption in appearance can be attained. Nietzsche finds something sublime in the way the pleasure to be had from the beauty of appearance can be experienced through the Apollonian. A different kind of sublime, however, is opened up through the Dionysian and the breakdown of cognitive forms it inaugurates. This is the sublime of horror. Nietzsche endeavours to give equal weight to the two forces or powers, and he does not follow Schopenhauer in simply arguing for a mystical suppression of the will; rather, he attempts a justification of the plane of appearance itself.

Nietzsche is conducting what is essentially a double argument in *The Birth of Tragedy*. On the one hand, we find a controversial argument about the origin and decline of Greek tragedy (sections 1–15); and, on the other hand, we encounter an impassioned tract in favour of a regeneration of contemporary German culture (sections 16–25). What links the two arguments together is the role Nietzsche ascribes to music. Greek tragedy is born of music, and Nietzsche places his hopes for cultural renewal on Wagnerian opera. In *The World as Will and Representation* Schopenhauer had argued that music was a unique art because of its non-representational character. Music can bypass the superficial and apparent world (a world of representation) and provide us with access to the world in its essence, the world as will. For Nietzsche the tragic cannot be deduced from the aesthetic category of appearance and the beautiful, but only on the basis of the spirit of music for only through this spirit do we encounter the joy experienced in the destruction of the individual.

In 1886 Nietzsche wrote an incisive critique of the book. He viewed it as 'image-mad and image-confused', as well as sentimental and 'saccharine to the point of effeminacy'. Upon its publication the work met with vehement rejection and denunciation by the community of philologists, and after being rejected by his mentor, Friedrich Ritschl, who had secured his post at Basel, Nietzsche was forced to admit that he had fallen from grace and become an ostracised figure. Nietzsche was entering a period of deep crisis. He was losing students from his classes, and within a few years he began to have serious doubts about Wagner as an artist and his support of the Wagner cause seriously waned.

The Birth of Tragedy has always had both detractors and supporters. In our own time it has been fiercely contested. In Nietzsche's valorisation of the Dionysian and the book's promulgation of an artist's metaphysics, Jürgen Habermas, one of the leading figures of the post-war intellectual landscape, sees a dangerous irrationalism and aestheticism, in which the Dionysian is sealed off from the world of both theoretical comprehension and the moral activity of everyday life. Whilst it affords access to a world of ecstasy, says Habermas, it does so at the price of a painful dissolution of the individual into amorphous nature. Other commentators, however, such as Peter Sloterdijk, argue that Nietzsche's text is best read as a work of the cultural avant-garde. Although it is the case that in the modern period the aesthetic has become divorced from the other areas of our existence, this means for Sloterdijk that the work of art is free to explore alternative modes of becoming a subject. He argues that the Dionysian is not simply realised in forgetful ecstasy but works to undermine an identity-bound perception of ourselves and secure the release of more fluid energies. There is a strong tradition in Western culture of conceiving individual identity in terms of notions of coherence, stability and fullness. Nietzsche's *The Birth of Tragedy*, Sloterdijk argues, shows this conception of human identity to be purely imaginary.

Nietzsche's thinking undergoes some fundamental changes after *The Birth of Tragedy* and the early period of 1872–6. Although art continues to play an important role in his thinking (it gets configured as 'the good will to appearance' that enables us to endure existence), the demands of knowledge and science are taken much more seriously. A new thinking of individuation takes place in Nietzsche's later texts, in which to be an individual is no longer to be condemned to a condition of metaphysical affliction. Nietzsche's views on the pain of existence also undergo significant development. In *Thus Spoke Zarathustra* what we suffer from as finite individuals is time's passing. In *On the Genealogy of Morality* our suffering stems from neither metaphysical nor existential sources but from the requirements of cultural formation and social differentiation. He no longer speaks of the cruelty of nature but rather views cruelty as an element in the development of social and ethical life. In spite of the transformations his thinking was to undergo after his first period of writing, Nietzsche remained attached to the Dionysian as a philosophy of life. Some insight into how Dionysos is conceived by Nietzsche in his late work will be provided in the final chapter.

2

HUMAN, ALL TOO HUMAN – HISTORICAL VERSUS METAPHYSICAL PHILOSOPHY

Chemistry of concepts and sensations. – Almost all the problems of philosophy once again pose the same form of question as they did two thousand years ago: how can something originate in its opposite, for example rationality in irrationality, the sentient in the dead, logic in unlogic, disinterested contemplation in covetous desire, living for others in egoism, truth in error? Metaphysical philosophy has hitherto surmounted this difficulty by denying that the one originates in the other and assuming for the more highly valued thing a miraculous source in the very kernel and being of the 'thing in itself'. Historical philosophy, on the other hand, which can no longer be separated from natural science, the youngest of all philosophical methods, has discovered in individual cases (and this will probably be the result in every case) that there are no opposites, except in the customary exaggeration of popular or metaphysical interpretations, and that a mistake in reasoning lies at the bottom of this antithesis: according to this explanation there exists, strictly speaking, neither an unegoistic action nor completely disinterested contemplation; both are only sublimations, in which the basic element seems almost to have dispersed and reveals itself only under the most painstaking observation. All we require, and what can be given us only now the individual sciences have attained their present level, is a *chemistry* of the moral, religious and aesthetic conceptions and sensations, likewise of all the agitations we experience within ourselves in cultural and social intercourse, and indeed even when we are alone: what if this chemistry would end up by revealing that in this domain too the most glorious colours are derived from base, indeed from despised materials? Will there be many who desire to pursue such researches? Mankind likes to put questions of origins and beginnings out of its mind: must one not be almost inhuman to detect in oneself a contrary inclination? –

Family failing of philosophers. – All philosophers have the common failing of starting out from man as he is now and thinking they can reach their goal through an analysis of him. They involuntarily think of 'man' as an *aeterna veritas*, as something that remains constant in the midst of all flux, as a sure measure of things. Everything the philosopher has declared about man is, however, at bottom no more than a testimony as to the man of a *very limited* period of time. Lack of historical sense is the family failing of all philosophers; many, without being aware of it, even take the most recent manifestation of man, such as has arisen under the impress of certain religions, even certain political events, as the fixed form from which one has to start out. They will not learn that man has become, that the faculty of cognition has become; while some of them would have it that the whole world is spun out of this faculty of cognition. Now, everything *essential* in the development of mankind took place in primeval times, long before the four thousand years we more or less know about; during these years mankind may well not have altered very much. But the philosopher here sees 'instincts' in man as he now is and assumes that these belong to the unalterable facts of mankind and to that extent could provide a key to the understanding of the world in general: the whole of teleology is constructed by speaking of the man of the last four millennia as of an *eternal* man towards whom all things in the world have had a natural relationship from the time he began. But everything has become: there are *no eternal facts*, just as there are no absolute truths. Consequently what is needed from now on is *historical philosophizing*, and with it the virtue of modesty.

Extract from *Human, All Too Human*, aphorisms 1 and 2

In 1878 Nietzsche published the first volume of *Human, All Too Human*, a book very different in tone and outlook from his first, and dedicated it to Voltaire, champion of the French Enlightenment. Wagner was repulsed by Nietzsche's new philosophical outlook and thought he had become deranged. In contrast to the Dionysian exultations and epiphanies of *The Birth of Tragedy*, Nietzsche now invites his reader to value small, unpretentious truths, to celebrate the science of physics for its modest explanations, and to abandon faith in all inspiration and knowledge acquired by miraculous means.

Soon after the book's publication Nietzsche's deteriorating health forced him to resign his position at the University of Basel, which thereafter granted him a small annual pension. Nietzsche had anyhow come to appreciate the extent to which the pursuit of his philosophical task was irreconcilable with academic life. He spent the next ten years of his sane life as a perpetual traveller, with periods of residence in Venice, Genoa, St Moritz, Rome, Sorrento and Nice. In the summer of 1881 he made his first trip to Sils-Maria in the Upper Engadine region of Switzerland, which was to become his regular summer residence. In a letter he wrote at the time to his amanuensis, Peter Gast, Nietzsche spoke of leading an extremely perilous life (intellectually speaking) and of being 'one of those machines which can explode'. The intensity of his feelings, he confided, made him shudder and laugh, weeping not sentimental tears but tears of joy. He would now oscillate between states of euphoria and depression.

The summer of 1881 was full of portents for Nietzsche. He discovered a precursor in Spinoza (1632–77) and only a few days after this discovery he had his experience of the idea of eternal recurrence which he jotted down on a piece of paper '6,000 feet beyond man and time'. In *Ecce Homo* he explains that one day, whilst on a walk through the woods beside the lake of Silvaplana, he stopped next to a 'mighty pyramidal block of stone', and 'then this idea came to me'. He calls eternal recurrence the highest formula of affirmation that can be attained. The affinity he felt with Spinoza was over a shared set of doctrines, including the denial of the notions of free will, purpose, a moral world order and evil, and the tendency of making knowledge the most powerful passion.

One other episode in Nietzsche's life that took place during this period needs to be mentioned. This is his friendship, often described as a platonic *ménage à trois*, with Paul Rée (1849–1901) and Lou Salomé (1861–1937). Rée was five years Nietzsche's junior, and was working on his doctoral thesis at the time Nietzsche first met him in 1873. He published two books in the 1870s – *Psychological Observations* (1875) and *On the Origin of Our Moral Sensations* (1877) – that served to inspire Nietzsche's turn to psychology in the mid-1870s. Rée was an atheist who held that religious experience was not a given fact but an interpretation that could be explained through psychology. He also argued that morality was not 'nature' but custom and that good and evil were simply conventions. Nietzsche admired what he called Rée's 'coldness', by which he meant his intellectual independence and clarity. For Rée the fact that existence lacked meaning became a source of despair; Nietzsche, by contrast, saw the same lack of meaning as the source of human freedom. It was Rée who, along with another friend, introduced Nietzsche to Salomé in April 1882. She was born in St Petersburg (her father was a Russian general and a Baltic German of Huguenot descent) and left Russia in September 1880 to study at the University of Zurich. She was soon to become a prolific writer, and was the author of the first serious study of Nietzsche. Later she became Rainer Maria Rilke's lover and confidante, and an esteemed friend of Sigmund Freud. The details of the unusual relationship between Salomé, Nietzsche and Rée, in which the two men independently proposed marriage to Salomé (she spurned both), cannot be traced here. Let it suffice to note that it tested Nietzsche's emotional powers of endurance to the limit. Ultimately, what is important about this painful episode in Nietzsche's life are the philosophical riches he brings out of it, notably his remarkable work *Thus Spoke Zarathustra* (1883–5). The relationship with Lou was over by October 1882 and the first part of *Thus Spoke Zarathustra* was written in ten days at the start of 1883.

Human, All Too Human bears the subtitle 'a book for free spirits'. In his reflections on this text in *Ecce Homo* Nietzsche says that the expression 'free spirit' needs to be heard in terms of a spirit that has become free. In other words, a process of self-liberation is involved, which includes a victory over idealism: where we see ideal things Nietzsche will see 'human, alas all too human things'. Human, all too human, as the title of a book and name of a project, amounts to the memorial of a crisis that compelled Nietzsche to impose on himself a rigorous self-discipline with regard to matters of knowledge. The free spirit is a relatively straightforward notion when he first articulates it, denoting a spirit that thinks differently from what would be expected based on their environment, class or dominant views of the age. Such a spirit has liberated itself from the fetters of tradition and has on its side the spirit of inquiry after truth which must eschew all faith and habit and demand only reasons. Although its actual sense does not significantly change as his work develops in the 1880s, the tasks demanded of it become more and more severe.

With the publication of *Human, All Too Human* in 1878 Nietzsche outlined an approach to philosophical questions that would inform all his subsequent work. It is what he called 'historical philosophising', and it clearly shows the influence exerted on his thinking by modern science, especially evolutionary theory (Darwin's great work, *The Origin of Species*, had been published in 1859). Nietzsche speaks of enacting on things the 'hammer blow of historical knowledge'. He persisted with the 'historical method', as he calls it, in *On the Genealogy of Morality*, and there are parts of *Twilight of the Idols* that bear a striking resemblance to the opening sections of *Human, All Too Human*. Nietzsche now dons the guise of an agnostic with regard to the question of whether a metaphysical world exists or not. There could be a metaphysical world but because we cannot chop off our own head all we can say is that it has a 'differentness' that is inaccessible to us; any ontology of it could only be a negative one. Moreover, knowledge of a metaphysical world would prove to be as inconsequential to us as the knowledge of the chemical analysis of water to someone in a boat facing a storm. Art, religion or morality do not provide us with access to another dimension of reality (as Nietzsche had argued in *The Birth of Tragedy* in the case of the Dionysian). We always find ourselves within a realm of representation and no intuition can take us any further. Furthermore, what we call the world is the result of numerous errors that result from the development of organic life. This collection of errors and fantasies also constitutes the treasure of a tradition – the value of humanity depends on it – and this gives rise to a conflict between our reliance on error and need for fantasy and the development of science and scientific truth.

In the opening section of *Human, All Too Human* Nietzsche focuses on the question of how something can originate in its opposite and sets up a contrast between 'metaphysical philosophy' and 'historical philosophy'. The former answers the question by appealing to a miraculous source such as a 'thing in itself' to explain the origin of something held to be of a higher value. This 'in itself' is taken by Nietzsche to denote something unconditioned that resides outside the conditions of life such as evolutionary change. The latter, by contrast, which Nietzsche insists can no longer be separated from the natural sciences (the youngest of all philosophical methods, he says), seeks to show that there are no opposites but that all things arise from and are implicated in a process of sublimation, hence his call for a 'chemistry of concepts and sensations' (chemistry being the science of change).

This historical mode of philosophising gives rise to a number of ideas that have proved seminal in modern thought: there are no unalterable facts of mankind; our faculty of cognition far from being the transcendental source or originator of our knowledge of the world (the reference is to Kant)[2] has itself evolved; and a society's order of rank concerning what it holds to be good and evil actions is constantly changing (*Human, All Too Human* 2 and 107). The human animal is the product of a prehistoric process going back thousands of years. What man is now is not what he has been destined to be from time immemorial. This aspect of Nietzsche's work, along with his later project of a genealogy of morality, exerted a deep influence on Foucault's celebrated, but also controversial, work on the history of reason and the formation of 'man' as a subject of scientific knowledge.

Nietzsche holds that the impulse to want certainties in the domain of first and last things is best regarded as a '*religious after-shoot*'. The first and last things refer to those questions of knowledge concerning the 'outermost regions': how did the universe begin? What is its purpose? It is only under the influence of ethical and religious sensations that these questions have acquired for us such a dreadful weightiness. They compel the eye to strain and where it encounters darkness it only makes things even darker. Where it proves impossible to establish certainties of any kind an entire moral–metaphysical world is constructed to fill this darkness. Various fantastical notions come to govern the way human beings see the world, which posterity is then asked to take seriously as true. This is why

carrying out an inquiry into the origins of ethical and religious sensations is such an important task. Its fundamental
objective is a deflationary one. We do not require certainties
with regard to the first and last things – what Nietzsche calls
'the furthest horizon' – in order to live a 'full and excellent
human life' (*The Wanderer and His Shadow* 16). He proposes
that we break with customary habits of thinking. In the face
of questions such as: what is the purpose of man? What is his
fate after death? How can man be reconciled with God?, it
should not be felt necessary to develop knowledge against
faith; rather we should practise indifference.

The position Nietzsche adopts on philosophical topics in
the opening of *Human, All Too Human* gets refined in his
subsequent writings as he continues to work on his tasks and
to develop a greater sense of their nature. These opening
aphorisms of *Human, All Too Human*, for example, are echoed
in a number of those which make up the opening chapter of
Beyond Good and Evil entitled 'On the Prejudices of
Philosophers'. Some new tasks are now added, including the
critique of morality that focuses on the value of values. An
inquiry into origins is not enough; rather, the question of
value must be reckoned with, and simply showing the lowly
origins of the highest things cannot do this. In addition, new
concepts come into play and are brought to bear on the critical tasks Nietzsche sets for knowledge, notably the will to
power. In *Beyond Good and Evil* Nietzsche argues that it is
necessary to wait 'for a new category of philosophers' to
arrive (*Beyond Good and Evil* 2). These philosophers yet to
come will not accept at face value the belief of the metaphysicians in the opposition of values. The taste and
inclination of these philosophers will be very different from
those which have hitherto guided philosophical inquiry. They
will ask some new questions: might truth arise out of error?

Might altruism be a form of egoism? Might the pure contemplation of the wise man arise out of covetous desire?

At the centre of Nietzsche's mature work is an attack on modes of thought, such as Platonism, which posit a dualism between a true world and a merely apparent one. The true world is held to be outside the order of time, change, plurality and becoming – it is a world of being – while the world of change, becoming and evolution is held to be a false world, one of error and mere semblance. In section 1 of '"Reason" in Philosophy' in *Twilight of the Idols* he argues that the peculiar idiosyncrasy of philosophers in general is their lack of historical sense and their hatred of the idea of becoming, what he calls their Egypticism: philosophers dehistoricise things and in the process mummify the concepts they are using to comprehend them. What has not been adequately dealt with are processes of life, such as death, change, procreation, growth, so that whatever truly has being is held not to become and what becomes is held to be nothing real and to lack being. In section 4 he notes how in metaphysics the most general and emptiest concepts – the absolute, the good, the true and the perfect – are posited as the highest and richest concepts. They must be presented as miraculous causes of themselves and be free of the contamination of growth and evolution. The thinnest and emptiest of all these concepts is that of God. In section 5 Nietzsche argues that the language of reason has led metaphysicians astray. Language emerged at the time of the most rudimentary form of psychology and scientific knowledge, and within it we can identify a crude fetishism which makes us think in certain ways that have now become habitual, such as positing the will as a cause of events and of action and a unified 'I' as the centre of our being in the world.

The philosophical tradition has continually overestimated

the importance of the role of consciousness in life. Nietzsche is convinced that the attempt to fathom inner processes and activity is hindered by the inability of language to grasp differentiation and by the imprecision in our observation. He states this strongly in aphorism 115 of *Daybreak* when he writes: '*We are none of us* that which we appear to be in accordance with the states for which alone we have consciousness and words.' Consciousness is 'a more or less fantastic commentary on an unknown, perhaps unknowable, but felt text' (*Daybreak* 129). For Nietzsche science shows us an alien world, one that is very different from how we imagine and think of the world when we describe our experiences and talk of our feelings and desires. He poses the question of whether we can learn to think and feel differently, and even dream more truly. The problem that this raises, however, is an immense and perhaps insuperable one: we necessarily interpret the world through our own psychical fictions and projections, and Nietzsche's innermost thinking of the world as will to power, which is a 'pre-form of life' he says in *Beyond Good and Evil* 36, cannot escape the charge of anthropomorphism. We don't have access to a pure ontological language that would tell us in neutral terms what the world is. To conceive the evolution of events taking place in the world in terms of a language of so-called pre-human affects, as Nietzsche does, is already to engage in an act of translation, as he himself fully acknowledges.

The development of Nietzsche's philosophical thinking presents some serious difficulties for the reader who wishes to make critical sense of his project. In his mature period (1885–8) it is clear that he does not wish to relinquish the specific tasks of philosophical thinking, which in part are tasks of elevation and ennoblement, and rest content with the pursuit of knowledge we find in science. He is highly critical of those he calls 'hodgepodge philosophers', such as modern positivists, who hold that facts rule the world and that science has overcome philosophy; and he laments the reduction of philosophy to the theory of knowledge as an act of shameful timidity (*Beyond Good and Evil* 204). In contrast to this ruination of philosophy he seeks to practise it as a discipline of 'real spiritual power' involving 'spiritual vision of real *depth*' (ibid., 252). However, he is equally critical of the continued attachment to metaphysics in modern German thought, notably in Kant. He insists that practical reason needs to be replaced by the intellectual conscience and demands that philosophy give up its priestly vocation by submitting itself to the rigorous tests of science (*The Anti-Christ* 12). His critical attitude towards Kant is a severe one because he thinks that in his construction of practical reason – where the classical ideas of metaphysics, such as God, free will and the immortality of the soul, gain a new legitimacy (although these ideas cannot satisfy the requirements of theoretical knowledge they are entitled to exist as postulates of practical reason, so satisfying what Nietzsche calls 'our heart's desire') – Kant had given up on the claims of scientific reason and buttressed the old morality and metaphysics with an irrational appeal to the sublime. Kant, Nietzsche says, gives us a higher reason designed specifically for the case where we are not supposed to bother about reason. And yet from 1883 onwards we find appearing in Nietzsche's writings a kind of metaphysics (largely centred on the thinking of life as will to power, which also serves as the principle of his mature historical method), and the positing of a new ideal (the superman is to become the new meaning of the earth).

Some commentators have argued that this shows that Nietzsche went on to develop his own 'Egypticism' and that he could not completely free philosophy from its priestly heritage. Nietzsche is in search of a mode of thinking that has moved beyond the old metaphysics and the old morality; and yet it is clear that something of the character of a sublime morality is at work in this movement and shows itself in all the fundamental ideas that we encounter in the mature and late texts, such as the eternal return, the superman and Dionysos. Some essential insight into each one of these and the work they are doing in his thinking will be offered in later chapters of this book.

3

NIETZSCHE'S CHEERFULNESS

How to understand our cheerfulness. – The greatest recent event –
that 'God is dead'; that the belief in the Christian God has become
unbelievable – is already starting to cast its first shadow over Europe.
To those few at least whose eyes – or the *suspicion* in whose eyes is
strong and subtle enough for this spectacle, some kind of sun seems
to have set; some old deep trust turned into doubt: to them, our
world must appear more autumnal, more mistrustful, stranger,
'older'. But in the main one might say: for many people's power of
comprehension, the event is itself far too great, distant, and out of
the way even for its tidings to be thought of as having arrived yet.
Even less may one suppose many to know at all *what* this event really
means – and, now that this faith has been undermined, how much
must collapse because it was built on this faith, leaned on it, had
grown into it – for example, our entire European morality. This long,
dense succession of demolition, destruction, downfall, upheaval that
now stands ahead: who would guess enough of it today to play the
teacher and herald of this monstrous logic of horror, the prophet of
deep darkness and an eclipse of the sun the like of which has probably never before existed on earth? Even we born guessers of riddles
who are so to speak on a lookout at the top of the mountain, posted
between today and tomorrow and stretched in the contradiction
between today and tomorrow, we firstlings and premature births of
the next century, to whom the shadows that must soon envelop
Europe really *should* have become apparent by now – why is it that

even we look forward to this darkening without any genuine involve-
ment and above all without worry and fear for *ourselves*? Are we
perhaps still not too influenced by the *most immediate consequences* of this event – and these immediate consequences, the
consequences for *ourselves*, are the opposite of what one might
expect – not at all sad and gloomy, but much more like a new and
barely describable type of light, happiness, relief, amusement,
encouragement, dawn . . . Indeed, at hearing the news that 'the old
god is dead', we philosophers and 'free spirits' feel illuminated by a
new dawn; our heart overflows with gratitude, amazement, forebod-
ings, expectation – finally the horizon seems clear again, even if not
bright; finally our ships may set out again, set out to face any
danger; every daring of the lover of knowledge is allowed again; the
sea, *our* sea, lies open again; maybe there has never been such an
'open sea'.

Extract from *The Gay Science*, aphorism 343

Everyone knows that Nietzsche proclaimed the death of God.
However, precisely what he meant by this requires interpretation. Nietzsche puts these words in the mouth of a madman
and has him announce them in a market square (in the original sketch of *The Gay Science* 125 the character of the
madman is played by a named persona – Zarathustra).
Nietzsche does not simply say 'God is dead' as if reporting
some scientific observation. He dramatises this event in order
to show its fateful character. The madman is, in fact, address-
ing the people as atheists who greet his news with incredulity
and ridicule simply because they would rest content with the
mere fact of God's death. As Walter Kaufmann noted,
Nietzsche's language in *The Gay Science* 125 is a religious one
with the picture being derived from the Gospels. Nietzsche
does not simply say 'God is dead' but has a madman declare
this *and* that 'we have killed him'. The statement is not a
metaphysical speculation about an ultimate reality, but a diag-
nosis of the state of European culture and its direction.

Nietzsche's 'gay science' seeks to introduce new experimental modes of thinking with regard to the questions we can pose about truth, knowledge and existence. He does not equate his project with an existing set of practices of knowledge, such as the natural sciences, but seeks to give expression to the full range of capacities of thought that the lover of knowledge must now cultivate. Walter Kaufmann suggested that the word 'gay' in Nietzsche's title should be heard in the sense of the unconventional, indicating a knowledge that defies convention and provides Nietzsche's 'immoralism' – the attempt to pursue questions and problems free of moral prejudices and fears – with its distinctive mood. Nietzsche's conception of the gay science was inspired in part by the Provençal knights and troubadours of the eleventh to fourteenth centuries who practised the art of courtly love. In *Ecce Homo* Nietzsche says that his attempt to 'dance over morality' expresses a perfect Provençalism. In *Beyond Good and Evil* 260 Nietzsche speaks of 'love as passion' and notes that this idea was invented by the 'Provençal knight-poets . . . inventive people of the *gai saber* to whom Europe owes so much'. One commentator has instructively defined the gay science in terms of a 'philosophical beatitude in which the most lucid and thus the least reassuring knowledge is accompanied by the most euphoric mood . . .'[3] This is precisely what is on display in the aphorism that heads this chapter.

In his preface to the second edition of *The Gay Science* (1887) Nietzsche says that the gay science signifies the saturnalia of a spirit who has resisted a long and terrible pressure or burden severely, coldly and without hope but who now is suddenly attacked by hope. In speaking of his recovery Nietzsche is not claiming to have found answers to questions that afflicted him in the past but rather to have discovered new and original things. The faith of this spirit is in 'tomorrow and the day after tomorrow'. The free spirit who practises the gay science has given up on the need for some finale to life and for a final state which can lead only to a craving for a beyond, an outside or an above. Self-liberation consists in liberation from one's own romanticism. Anticipation of the future and of the new cannot simply be that of the distressed and impotent. Nietzsche invokes the ideal of a spirit who knows how to play with all that has hitherto been called holy, good and divine, which is the ideal of 'human, superhuman well-being and benevolence', one that will often appear inhuman when it confronts all earthly seriousness to date (*The Gay Science* 382). Nietzsche is in search of a community of free spirits who will not be oppressed by the weight of the past but who are able to feel '*very light*' with respect to their will to knowledge (380). He stresses that the key question 'is how light or heavy we are', which is 'the problem of our "specific gravity"'.

Aphorism 343 opens Book Five of *The Gay Science*, which carries the title 'We Fearless Ones', and is devoted to the topic of Nietzsche's kind of cheerfulness. The aphorism speaks of an event that can fairly be considered the greatest of all recent ones and in order to convey the full impact of it Nietzsche deploys some highly colourful imagery: a setting sun, an eclipsed sun and a world becoming autumnal. This event will cast a shadow; its actual eventful character will not be perceived and recognised as such by everyone as there are many for whom it will still appear as distant; and much harder to grasp for many is the meaning of this event. It is not only that a religious faith has collapsed; rather, everything that has been built on this faith will now be shaken to the core. At this point in the aphorism, where we move from an opening depiction of a sun that has set to one where the sun has been eclipsed, Nietzsche begins to introduce a series of questions that serves to implicate the reader more and more in what is being revealed.

In the final part of the aphorism Nietzsche seems to be indicating that the free spirits have been patiently waiting for this event and are in some deep sense prepared for it. He speaks, for example, of their particular love of knowledge being possible once again, so indicating that some kind of return is taking place. It is not perhaps the first time that the horizon has become clear. Nietzsche, however, cannot hold back from expressing the sense of liberation that overwhelms him, and so chooses to draw the aphorism to a close by wondering whether there has ever been such a sea as that which now opens up before us. However, a note of caution is immediately sounded in the very next aphorism, entitled 'How we are still too pious', where he makes it clear that some new and highly demanding tasks now face all free-spirited philosophers and lovers of knowledge.

This will be looked at in the next chapter. Let me devote the rest of this chapter to clarifying the death of God and Nietzsche's cheerfulness. The notion of the death of God and the dying gods was one familiar to the young Nietzsche. In a note of 1870 he declares that he believes in the ancient German saying that 'All gods must die'. Even earlier than this, in a letter of 1862 to some school friends, he writes that the becoming man of God indicates that we should not search for blessedness in the infinite but ground our heaven on earth. The delusion of a world beyond serves only to cast the human in a false relation to the earthly world. Nietzsche is by no means the first philosopher to speak of the death of God. The philosopher Hegel writes of it in his *Philosophy of Religion* (1827), citing a Lutheran hymn of 1641 which contains the phrase 'God himself is dead'. In Nietzsche the event denotes two things. On the one hand, it names the death of the symbolic God – that is, the death of the particular God of Christianity. Although this God has helped to breed a pathological hatred of the human animal and the earth, it has also served to protect the human will from theoretical and practical nihilism. On the other hand, it means that the God of theologians, philosophers and some scientists, that is, the God that serves as a guarantor that the universe is not devoid of structure, order and purpose, is also dead. In section 109 of *The Gay Science*, a long section that comes immediately after the very short one where Nietzsche first mentions the death of God (108), he makes clear that there are shadows of God that must be vanquished. There are a number of things we need to beware of, such as, for example, thinking of the universe as either a living being or a machine, thinking that there are laws of nature when there are only necessities, thinking that death is opposed to life when the living is simply a rare type of what is dead, replacing the fiction of God with a cult of matter, and so on. Nietzsche argues, in short, that we face a situation of difficult knowledge simply because we realise that none of our aesthetic and moral judgements applies to the universe. At the end of this aphorism he calls for these shadows of God to stop darkening the human mind, which can come about only through the removal of God from nature.

For Nietzsche humanity has reached a point in history where belief in God has become unbelievable. This is precisely how he states the issue in the aphorism we are reading. It is not necessary for atheists to engage in counter-proofs of God's existence simply because the problem is not a metaphysical one. In *The Gay Science* 357 Nietzsche acknowledges Schopenhauer as the first uncompromising atheist among German thinkers, someone for whom the ungodly character of existence counted as something palpable and beyond dispute.

Schopenhauer's whole integrity rests on the fact that he became indignant when anyone tried to beat around the bush on this issue. Unconditional and honest atheism, Nietzsche says, represents the victory of a European conscience that has been won with great difficulty; it is 'the most fateful act of two thousand years of discipline for truth that in the end forbids itself the *lie* of faith in God'. Ironically, what triumphs over God is Christian morality itself and its concept of truthfulness, that is, its pursuit of intellectual and moral cleanliness. The confessor's refinement of Christian conscience eventually sublimates itself into a scientific conscience which is an intellectual conscience 'at any price'. What is now over includes: looking at nature as if it gave proof of the goodness and care of a god; interpreting history in terms of some divine reason and the testimony of a moral world order; and interpreting one's experiences piously as if they were designed and ordained for the sake of the salvation of one's soul.

Nietzsche clearly wishes to promote the cultivation of a new spiritual maturity that will enable us to deal adequately with the new situation in which we find ourselves and not be overcome by disillusionment and despair. In his earlier text, *Human, All Too Human*, he mentions the need in a post-metaphysical age for the requisite temperament, namely, a cheerful soul (*Human, All Too Human* 34). Indeed, throughout his writings, from first to last, Nietzsche can be found wrestling with the meaning of his cheerfulness. The German word in *The Gay Science* 343 is *Heiterkeit*, used ironically in the sense of 'that's going to be fun', as for example, when out for a walk, you watch a huge black cloud approaching and foresee getting drenched. You go on the walk even though you know that risks are involved. The way in which Nietzsche presents his cheerfulness in this aphorism clearly contains something of this sense, indicating a spirit of adventure and fearlessness with regard to the pursuit of knowledge. His cheerfulness has many hidden depths and dimensions. It explains the peculiar sense of distance he himself feels in relation to the monstrous event of the death of the Christian God.

Nietzsche foregrounded cheerfulness as a theme in his first published book, *The Birth of Tragedy*. There he mentions the need to secure the proper comprehension of the 'serious and important concept of "Greek cheerfulness"' (*The Birth of Tragedy* 9). His view is that a misunderstanding of this concept is to be found everywhere today where it is encountered in a state of unendangered comfort. What is missing is any appreciation of the depths of being from which the Greek concept emerged and any sense of the tragic insights that informed and inspired it. In *Schopenhauer as Educator* (1874) Nietzsche is keen to show that there are two quite different types of cheerful thinkers. The true thinker always cheers and refreshes, whether he is being serious or humorous, and he does so by expressing his insight not with trembling hands and eyes filled with tears but with courage and strength, and as a victor. What cheers most profoundly, he adds, is that the true thinker enables us to 'behold the victorious god with all the monsters he has combated' (*Schopenhauer as Educator* 2). There is no point in a thinker assuming the guise of a teacher of new insights and new truths unless he has courage, is able to communicate, and knows the costs of what has been conquered. By contrast the cheerfulness of mediocre writers and quick thinkers makes us feel miserable. This kind of cheerful thinker, he says, does not see the sufferings and monsters he purports to see and combat. The cheerfulness of the shallow thinker needs to be exposed because it tries to convince us that things are easier than they really are. The cheerfulness we can respond to must come from one who has thought most deeply and who loves what is most living.

Nietzsche holds that for our thinking to be of any worth the things we think about must cause us to suffer. We must love our problems, for only in this way do we gain a sense of their depth and weight. This is a peculiar and distinctive feature of his approach to philosophical thinking. In the preface to the second edition of *The Gay Science* he writes that a thinker who has traversed many different kinds of health has gone through an equal number of philosophies, and philosophy is nothing other than this art of transfiguration by which the thinker transposes his states into a spiritual form and distance. Contrary to popular imagination a philosopher is not a thinking frog or simply a registering mechanism with their innards removed. Thought has to be given birth to out of the suffering and trials of life, and then endowed with 'blood, heart, fire, pleasure, passion, agony, conscience, fate and catastrophe'. Life, says Nietzsche, means essentially this – to transform all that we are and become into light and flame, including everything that wounds us. Out of various exercises in self-mastery one emerges as different and with more questions than one was prepared to entertain before. It is certain that our trust in life has gone, and gone for ever, simply because life has become a problem for us. Nietzsche counsels us, however, that we should not jump to the conclusion that this necessarily makes us gloomy. Love of life is still possible, but we now love differently. It can be compared to the 'love for a woman that causes doubts in us'.

Taking delight in the problem of life entails a highly spiritualised thinking, one that has conquered fear and gloominess. Nietzsche's cheerfulness stems from his experiences of knowledge, including the experience of disillusionment and despair that can result from the practice of the love of knowledge – this is the long pressure that needs to be resisted. He speaks of gay or joyful science as a reward – for example, 'a reward for a long, brave, diligent, subterranean seriousness . . .' (*On the Genealogy of Morality* preface 7). Knowledge is to be conceived in terms of a 'world of dangers and victories in which heroic feelings . . . find places to dance and play'. He posits as a principle, '*Life as a means to knowledge*' in which the pursuit of knowledge is not to be conducted in a spirit of duty or as a calamity or trickery (*The Gay Science* 324). He speaks of the human intellect as a 'clumsy, gloomy, creaking machine' and of how the human being always seems to lose its good spirits when it thinks by becoming too serious (*The Gay Science* 327). He wants to teach the intellect how it does not have to be such a machine and to challenge the prejudice that would hold that, where laughter and gaiety inform thinking, then this thinking is good for nothing. Nietzsche continues to speak of his cheerfulness in later works. In *Ecce Homo*, for example, he writes of being 'cheerful among nothing but hard truths' (*Ecce Homo* 'Why I Write Such Good Books' 3).

In *The Gay Science* 125 the madman asks whether we must not now become gods ourselves to be worthy of this event of God's death. There has never been a greater deed, he says, 'and whoever will be born after us will, for the sake of this deed, be part of a higher history than all history hitherto'.

Within a few years of Nietzsche writing this parable the problem of nihilism came to dominate his thoughts. As Walter Kaufmann noted, how to escape nihilism – which seems involved both in the assertion of God's existence (since it robs the earth of its value) and in the denial of it (since this seems to rob everything of meaning and value) – is Nietzsche's most persistent problem. We find this acknowledged by Nietzsche in *The Gay Science* 357, where he writes: 'As we thus reject the Christian interpretation and condemn its "meaning" as counterfeit, *Schopenhauer's* question immediately comes at us in a terrifying way: *Does existence have any meaning at all?*'

Nietzsche thought that a few centuries would be required before this question could be heard in its full depth. In the texts of his late period, such as *The Anti-Christ*, Nietzsche attempts to force a resolution of this problem of meaning by providing an answer to the question (which is his question): to what end shall 'man' as a whole, and no longer as a people or a race, be raised and disciplined? This will be looked at in chapter nine.

4

ON TRUTH AND KNOWLEDGE

Origin of knowledge. – Through immense periods of time, the intellect produced nothing but errors; some of them turned out to be
useful and species-preserving; those who hit upon or inherited them
fought their fight for themselves and their progeny with greater luck.
Such erroneous articles of faith, which were passed on by inheritance
further and further, and finally almost became part of the basic
endowment of the species, are for example: that there are enduring
things; that there are identical things; that there are things, kinds of
material, bodies; that a thing is what it appears to be; that our will is
free; that what is good for me is also good in and for itself. Only very
late did the deniers and doubters of such propositions emerge; only
very late did truth emerge as the weakest form of knowledge. It
seemed that one was unable to live with it; that our organism was
geared for its opposite: all its higher functions, the perceptions of
sense and generally every kind of sensation, worked with those basic
errors that had been incorporated since time immemorial. Further,
even in the realm of knowledge those propositions became the norms
according to which one determined 'true' and 'untrue' down to the
most remote areas of pure logic. Thus the *strength* of knowledge lies
not in its degree of truth, but in its age, its embeddedness, its character as a condition of life. Where life and knowledge seem to
contradict each other, there was never any serious fight to begin
with; denial and doubt were simply considered madness. Those
exceptional thinkers, like the Eleatics, who still posited and clung to

the opposites of the natural errors, believed in the possibility of also *living* this opposite: they invented the sage as the man of unchange-ability, impersonality, universality of intuition, as one and all at the same time, with a special capacity for that inverted knowledge; they had the faith that their knowledge was at the same time the principle of *life*. But in order to be able to claim all this, they had to *deceive* themselves about their own state: they had fictitiously to attribute to themselves impersonality and duration without change; they had to misconstrue the nature of the knower, deny the force of impulses in knowledge, and generally conceive reason as a completely free, self-originated activity. They closed their eyes to the fact that they, too, had arrived at their propositions in opposition to what was considered valid or from a desire for tranquillity or sole possession or sover-eignty. The subtler development of honesty and scepticism finally made also these people impossible; even their life and judgements proved dependent on the ancient drives and fundamental errors of all sentient existence. This subtler honesty and scepticism arose wher-ever two conflicting propositions seemed to be *applicable* to life because both were compatible with the basic errors, and thus where it was possible to argue about the greater or lesser degree of *useful-ness* for life; also wherever new propositions showed themselves to be not directly useful, but at least also not harmful, as expressions of an intellectual play impulse, and innocent and happy like all play. Gradually the human brain filled itself with such judgements and convictions; and ferment, struggle, and lust for power developed in this tangle. Not only utility and delight, but also every kind of drive took part in the fight about the 'truths'; the intellectual fight became an occupation, attraction, profession, duty, dignity – knowledge and the striving for the true finally took their place as a need among the other needs. Henceforth, not only faith and conviction, but also scrutiny, denial, suspicion, and contradiction were a *power*; all 'evil' instincts were subordinated to knowledge and put in its service and took on the lustre of the permitted, honoured, useful and finally the eye and the innocence of the *good*. Thus knowledge became a part of life and, as life, a continually growing power, until finally knowledge and the ancient basic errors struck against each other, both as life, both as power, both in the same person. The thinker – that is now the being in whom the drive to truth and those life-preserving errors are fighting their first battle, after the drive to truth has *proven* itself to be a life-preserving power, too. In relation to the significance of this battle, everything else is a matter of indifference: the ultimate question about the condition of life is posed here, and the first attempt is made here to answer the question through experiment. To what extent can truth stand to be incorporated? – that is the question; that is the experiment.

Extract from *The Gay Science*, aphorism 110

Nietzsche's statements on truth have perplexed his commentators. He is notorious for claims such as: life is not an argument in favour of truth since the conditions of life might include error (*The Gay Science* 121), man's truths might simply be his irrefutable errors (*The Gay Science* 265), and to admit untruth as a condition of life is to place oneself beyond good and evil (*Beyond Good and Evil* 4). Many commentators lose their patience with these riddles since they expect a philosopher to speak only the plain truth about truth. In defence of Nietzsche's playfulness – and as always this playfulness belies a deadly seriousness – it could be said that the job of the philosopher is to unsettle our fixed certainties and challenge our convictions. Nietzsche holds that there are no stronger convictions than the ones bound up with our belief in truth.

One of Nietzsche's earliest meditations on this subject is entitled 'On the Pathos of Truth' (1872). The title shows the extent to which he approaches truth in terms of our feelings about it (our belief in truth and our desire for it). In the early writings we encounter claims such as the following: there is a tragic conflict between our need for truth and our need for illusion; considered as an unconditional duty, our drive to truth proves itself to be a hostile power and could even destroy the world; truth kills and, in fact, kills itself when it recognises that its foundation is error; everything that is good and beautiful depends on illusion: 'Truthfulness, as the foundation of all compacts, and the prerequisite for the survival of the human species, is a eudemonistic demand: it is opposed by the knowledge that the supreme welfare lies in illusions.'[4] Nietzsche is taking truth to denote an unconditional power of knowledge and questioning it on this basis. He speaks of error because he thinks that our knowledge is of necessity characterised by imprecision, partialness and relativity. In his late writings Nietzsche argues that the categories of reason have their basis in our biological needs as a species, which are needs for security, control of the environment, and quick understanding on the basis of signs (*The Will to Power* 513). We comprehend a certain amount of reality in order to become master of it; the accumulation of experience takes place through the regularity of our perceptions and through knowledge of what is constant and calculable. We have no right to suppose that what proves useful in the preservation of a species like ours provides us with a proof of truth.

Truth has no single meaning in Nietzsche's writings. Sometimes it takes an existential form, while at other times it is presented in epistemological terms, in which the issue at stake is whether our categories of thought correspond to the world or whether they first enable us to construct and fabricate a world that we can then relate to in empirical terms. This is why he suggests that our categories and judgements of thought cannot be said to be 'true' and may indeed be 'false' (this is clearly a complicated assessment to make). On the existential front, where we are dealing with the arduous path to self-knowledge, Nietzsche will declare error to be blindness and cowardice and state that the measure of a person's value lies in how much truth they dare and can endure. We can move forward in knowledge only by being severe against ourselves. Nietzsche is holding to what we might think is an impossible position. On the one hand, the acquisition of self-knowledge necessitates the practice of truth; on the other hand, it is not possible to live in truth all the time and truth can never be an adequate medium of life. What is clear is that for Nietzsche truth, however it is conceived, has no metaphysical status. This claim is part of his commitment to 'perspectivism', which put simply is the view that entities exist only within a perspective and a horizon of interpretation. In *Beyond Good and Evil* 34 he argues that life is possible only on the basis of 'perspectivist assessments and appearances' (see also *The Gay Science* 374).

In this aphorism on the 'origin of knowledge'[5] we find Nietzsche developing an evolutionary account of the emergence of truth and asking some novel questions concerning the value we put on it. We exist today in a situation where knowledge itself has become a part of life. A preoccupation with truth actually appeared late in the evolution of human life and was for a long time to be the weakest form of knowledge on account of the fact that humans found it hard to endure. In the story Nietzsche is telling in this aphorism, this was owing to the fact that for the greater part of its evolutionary history the human animal has survived, prospered even, by incorporating a set of basic errors which became for it a set of 'erroneous articles of faith', such as that there are identical and enduring things and that things are what we immediately take them to be.

In the section that follows *The Gay Science* 110 he presents a quasi-Darwinian account of the origins and development of our basic ways of thinking. For example, to be able to think all the time in terms of identity proves helpful in the struggle for survival since it means things in the environment can be recognised and acted upon with speed. To see only perpetual change everywhere would be disastrous for the evolution of a species of animal. As Nietzsche points out, 'the beings who did not see exactly had a head start over those who saw everything "in a flux"' (*The Gay Science* 111). What has so far determined the strength or power of knowledge is not its degree of truth, as we might suppose, but rather its character as a condition of life. And wherever life and knowledge came into conflict, denial and doubt were taken to be expressions of madness. A new situation has now come into being in which the quest for knowledge and the striving for the true are recognised as powerful needs. Nietzsche brings the aphorism to a close by saying that the thinker today is 'the being in whom the drive to truth and those life-preserving errors are fighting their first battle'. Such a battle is now taking place because the striving for the true has also shown itself to be a life-preserving and life-enhancing power. In order to make further progress with truth it is necessary to conduct an experiment. This experiment will be one in a new form of incorporation.

The German word for incorporation (*Einverleibung*), like the English one, literally means a taking into the body (*Leib*). The notion clearly refers to a body taking into itself something from outside (this could be a simple life form such as a protoplasm or a more complex kind of organism such as ourselves, a society, a race of people, and so on). For Nietzsche everything that exists, if it is the result of evolutionary processes, includes within it alien material. Bodies do not evolve by establishing closed or fixed boundaries between themselves, between an inside and an outside; if this were the case nothing could, in fact, evolve. This means that a body does not have an identity that is fixed once and for all, but is essentially informed by a plastic and adaptive power, one capable of profound change (this is what Nietzsche denotes when he posits life as 'will to power', conceived as a desire in all living things for growth and expansion). Such change takes place through processes of assimilation and incorporation. All bodies have to learn to adapt through change since the rules of what can and cannot be assimilated are not given in evolution (although there are clearly struggles for power and of fitness). On this point Nietzsche is in agreement with Spinoza who argued that we do not know what a body can do (*Ethics* III, Proposition 2, Scholium).

With respect to truth, the experiment Nietzsche has in mind is one of finding out just what is involved in learning to live in the space or horizon of it. To ingest truth does not so much mean incorporating a set of specific or actual truths; rather, we need to think of a set of practices of truthfulness, such as permanent scepticism, suspension of belief, doubt, holding things at a distance and subjecting them to scrutiny, etc. Hitherto human beings have incorporated, or assimilated, only basic errors that are rooted in conditions of adaptive existence. Nietzsche is bothered by two insights: first, that error seems to be basic to our animal existence and so cannot be easily overcome; and, second, that truth is an intrinsically anthropological concept and so has no meaning outside of the conditions of human life (conditions of preservation and growth). Nietzsche clarifies his position on truth, conceived in terms of a mode of existence and as a 'will to truth', in his writings of 1887 where he undertakes a quite extraordinary and disquieting style of questioning (*The Gay Science* 344; *On the Genealogy of Morality* III, 23–7). This will, he says, is to be tentatively called into question and a critique performed.

In the third essay of *On the Genealogy of Morality* Nietzsche names modern science as the most recent and noblest manifestation of an idea that he regards as the only ideal so far developed by man and that he is seeking to question. This is what he calls the ascetic ideal, which I shall examine more fully in chapter nine. The fact that Nietzsche speaks of science as its most noble manifestation is not insignificant. He tells us that he does not wish to spoil the pleasure that its honest workers take in their craft and that he too takes delight in their work. Nevertheless, he maintains that science is a hiding place for all kinds of 'ill-humour', 'nagging worms' and 'bad conscience' (*On the Genealogy of Morality* III, 23). In accordance with the German word for science (*Wissenschaft*) Nietzsche does not restrict his criticism to the natural sciences but extends it to any disciplined practice of knowledge. In section 26, for instance, he takes modern historiography as an example and takes issue with it for wishing to be a mirror of reality. Modern science not only rejects all teleology (the focus on things having ultimate purposes and ends), but also scorns playing the judge, affirms as little as it denies, and is content with merely asserting and describing. Nietzsche argues that 'All of this is ascetic to a high degree; but to an even higher degree it is *nihilistic*, make no mistake about it!' (*On the Genealogy of Morality* III, 26). As a 'genuine philosophy of reality' modern science has the courage to be itself and finds itself well able to get by 'without God, the beyond and the virtues of denial' (ibid., 23). Nietzsche contends, however, that those who advocate science along these lines are simply indulging in 'propagandistic chatter' and those who currently trumpet reality as the object of knowledge are really 'bad musicians'. Their voices, he says, 'do *not* come from the depths, the abyss of scientific conscience does *not* speak from them' (ibid.). What is this abyss?

Science lacks an ideal beyond itself, such as the passion of great faith that would give its pursuit of knowledge a goal and a will. Science refuses to acknowledge that the practice of knowledge has a necessary and vital basis in interpretation and everything that is essential to it. Here Nietzsche names 'forcing, adjusting, shortening, omitting, filling-out, inventing, falsifying . . .' The fact that our knowledge will always be implicated in a perspectival selection is not to be taken as a

simple objection to it. Nietzsche takes issue with modern science because it is fundamentally dishonest about its pursuit of
knowledge; in reality it makes use of all those things he enu-
merates as essential to interpretation. Nietzsche insists that
knowledge without presuppositions is unimaginable. In order
for knowledge to win a direction, a philosophy or a 'faith' of
some kind has to inform it (*On the Genealogy of Morality* III,
24). Instead of confronting itself, science chooses to deny
itself and thus allows itself to be placed in the service of an
existing power.

Nietzsche calls for a critique of the will to truth. This does
not denote a solely negative task. We need to hear the word
critique in a specific sense. It is bound up, in part, with Kant's
original conception of critique as that which seeks to determine the scope and boundaries of something (in Kant's case
this is pure reason, practical reason and judgement). We might
want to propose that science is in need of a justification (what
is its *raison d'être*?), but here we cannot assume that there can,
in fact, be one. Instead, Nietzsche proposes that truth be considered a problem: 'From the very moment that faith in the
God of the ascetic ideal is denied, *there is a new problem as well*:
that of the *value* of truth' (ibid.). The free spirit is not truly
free until it learns the need to question the belief in truth and
knows how to question this belief. This is why he states that
to be a nihilist, an immoralist, or an Anti-Christ is not
enough: all these types remain idealists of knowledge until
they know how to question the will to truth and perform a
critique of it.

The issue of incorporation also features in an important
way in Nietzsche's conception of the tasks of self-knowledge,
including learning how to love oneself. The free spirit is a
spirit that knows how to digest knowledge and live on a diet
of it. The spirit that Nietzsche opposes is the one he names as

the spirit of gravity. This is a spirit that is overburdened with the weight of knowledge and of existence. Its need to chew and digest everything reveals a swinish nature. The spirit of gravity is one that does not know how to incorporate knowledge, that is, how to digest it and regulate it. Love of oneself as a finite human being is essential: 'One must learn to love oneself with a sound and healthy love, so that one may endure it with oneself and not go roaming about . . .' (*Thus Spoke Zarathustra*, 'The Spirit of Gravity', 2). This is love of oneself as the finest of all arts, requiring subtlety and patience. It is not so much that life is hard to bear, but rather that the human animal finds it hard to live with itself: it has to learn how to regulate its many conflicting desires and digest what happens to it, including its experiences of life.

Nietzsche is convinced that to want truth at any price is a sign of bad taste and a piece of youthful madness. The spirit that has become free has done so by learning an important lesson: the need to keep knowledge in bounds (*The Anti-Christ*, Foreword). In the preface to *The Gay Science* Nietzsche says we should not want to know everything or want to see everything naked. The complex task he sets for the spirit that seeks to become free is that of becoming superficial 'out of profundity'. At the end of a long aphorism in *Beyond Good and Evil* (230) he rails against metaphysical bird-catchers who would like to swoop our spirit away to other worlds by teaching the human animal that it is of a different origin from the rest of nature and something higher. He then quizzes himself and his readers: if knowledge, even at its deepest and most sublime, never takes us beyond human vanity, and we now translate the human back into nature, so as 'to master the many conceited and overly enthusiastic interpretations and secondary meanings that to date have been scrawled and painted over the eternal original text *homo natura*', why should we bother with it? Is it not simply a crazy project? For Nietzsche, the project of knowledge is worth bothering with because learning transforms us (*Beyond Good and Evil* 231). It is not simply that the philosopher is someone who provides food for thought; rather the philosopher shows that thought is food, just as spirit is a stomach (230): 'it acts as all nourishment does, doing more than just "keeping us going" – as physiologists know' (231). The problems we attempt to solve with solutions that inspire in us strong beliefs are only footprints on the way to self-knowledge and on this path we necessarily encounter, and at a very deep level, our own great stupidity.

5

ON MEMORY AND FORGETTING

To breed an animal *which is able to make promises* – is that not precisely the paradoxical task which nature has set herself with regard to humankind? Is it not the real problem *of* humankind? . . . The fact that this problem has been solved to a large degree must seem all the more surprising to the person who can fully appreciate the opposing force, *forgetfulness*. Forgetfulness is not just a *vis inertiae*, as superficial people believe, but is rather an active ability to suppress, positive in the strongest sense of the word, to which we owe the fact that what we simply live through, experience, take in, no more enters our consciousness during digestion (one could call it spiritual ingestion) than does the thousand-fold process which takes place with our physical consumption of food, our so-called ingestion. To shut the doors and windows of consciousness for a while; not to be bothered by the noise and battle with which our underworld of serviceable organs work with and against each other; a little peace, a little *tabula rasa* of consciousness to make room for something new, above all for the nobler functions and functionaries, for ruling, predicting, predetermining (our organism runs along oligarchic lines, you see) – that, as I said, is the benefit of active forgetfulness, like a doorkeeper or guardian of mental order, rest and etiquette: from which we can immediately see how there could be no happiness, cheerfulness, hope, pride, *immediacy*, without forgetfulness. The person in whom this apparatus of suppression is damaged, so that it stops working,

can be compared (and not just compared –) to a dyspeptic; he
cannot 'cope' with anything . . .
    Extract from *On the Genealogy of Morality*, essay 2, aphorism 1

In this chapter I want to examine what Nietzsche says about
memory and forgetting in this opening section of the second
essay of *On the Genealogy of Morality*, which is devoted to an
analysis of '"guilt", "bad conscience" and related matters',
and link it to reflections we find on this topic across his writings. He approaches memory as a problem of pathology, that
is, as bound up with issues of health and sickness, of a strong
will and an ill-will. Not surprisingly we find that questions of
incorporation and digestion are at the centre of his reflections.
For Nietzsche memory is not a formal organ or abstract faculty; rather, it is best conceived in terms of a diffuse function
with a physiological substrate. Memory is affective in nature,
being related to the drives. One commentator has suggested
that in Nietzsche the return of a memory refers to the time
when latent life-experiences that have survived in the unconscious erupt into consciousness, which is a clear anticipation
of Sigmund Freud's (1856–1939) psychoanalytic insights.[6]
Indeed, Nietzsche will say that it is not an 'I' or ego that
awakens memories but an 'it'.

The second essay of *On the Genealogy of Morality* begins
with the 'problem of humankind': the human is an animal
that has developed the capacity to make promises, and
Nietzsche regards this as a paradoxical task that nature has set
itself in the case of man and the real problem concerning
him. This capacity can be taken to be significant because
through it the human animal becomes an animal of time.
When one makes a promise one places oneself in a relationship with time and holds oneself to account for one's deeds
through a reckoning and calculation of it. At the end of the

section Nietzsche draws our attention to what must first take place before we become creatures of time and feel we have a degree of control over the future (the future itself comes into existence as a form of time with all of this): learning how to distinguish between what happens by accident and what happens by design, the capacity to think causally and to view the future as the present and anticipate it, and so on. In order to become an animal that can compute and calculate, the human being must have first become something '*reliable, regular, automatic*' in its own self-image. This is what Nietzsche goes on to explore in the sections that follow, in which he discusses the role played by the 'morality of custom', the 'social straitjacket', and a mnemotechnics in the long history of how the feeling of responsibility originated in us.

In his *The Uses and Disadvantages of History for Life* (1874) Nietzsche is already approaching fundamental questions of knowledge – in this case historical knowledge – out of a concern with digestion and spiritual health and vitality. In this meditation Nietzsche takes issue with the acute 'historical sense' of modern human beings, arguing that there is a degree of '*sleeplessness, of rumination, of the historical sense, which is harmful and ultimately fatal to the living thing*' (*The Uses and Disadvantages of History for Life* 1). In short, 'it is impossible to *live* at all without forgetting'. To determine this degree, so as to set the boundary by which the past is to be forgotten, requires knowledge of the plastic power of a human being and of a people or culture. This power refers to the capacity to develop out of oneself in one's own way and is a capacity for incorporation, 'to transform and incorporate into oneself what is past and foreign, to heal wounds, to replace what has been lost, to recreate broken moulds' (ibid.). In one sense it is a redemptive project, but one that is guided by the need for a principle of selection. The selection of time takes place for the sake of the future, to allow the future to take place. Knowledge of our power along these lines is necessary simply because without it we can perish from experiences, including a single experience or a single painful event. A strong and fruitful health can only come into being when bounded by a horizon. Nietzsche posits this as a universal law of the living. He writes: 'Cheerfulness, the good conscience, the joyful deed, confidence in the future – all of them depend, in the case of an individual as of a nation, on the existence of a line dividing the bright and discernible from the unilluminable and dark; on one's being just as able to forget at the right time as to remember at the right time . . .' (ibid.). A human being that did not possess the power of forgetting would no longer believe in its own being and lose himself in the stream of becoming. Forgetting is thus 'essential for the life of everything organic'.

Memory is not just a neutral recollection of events and things that have happened to us. It is also bound up with our affective or emotional life. The things of the past haunt us, have the potential to unsettle us, and remind us of experiences we have forgotten and wish to forget. Life is full of mummies, ghosts and phantoms – a whole series of people and places that exist for us as virtual objects. This tells us something significant about memory itself: it has an existence independent of our will. Memories can come back to us in an unsuspected manner, perhaps triggered, as the novelist Marcel Proust found, by an accidental encounter with a smell or a taste, which then opens up for us an entire forgotten world we once inhabited. This return of memory in an involuntary fashion can bring both great joy and tremendous anguish.[7]

This is something Nietzsche fully appreciated: 'One must revise one's ideas about memory' (*The Will to Power* 502). We are tempted to assume a 'soul' that lies outside time and which then reproduces and recognises itself in its memories. This, however, is to misunderstand the nature of ourselves as beings of memory – namely, the extent, Nietzsche says, to which 'that which is experienced lives on "in the memory"' – so we cannot help it if things come back to us simply because the will is inactive in this case, as it is in the emergence of any thought. Within the domain of conscious perception there necessarily takes place a selection of memory in accordance with the needs of the present. Only those memories considered to be useful to a current action are selected and allowed to enter consciousness. This does not mean, however, that memories simply get eroded with the passage of time. It is rather that memory as a whole exists in its own peculiar mode of being (inactive, unconscious and virtual) and particular memories can assert themselves against our will. Things that we thought were dead and buried can suddenly and unexpectedly return to life. One reason why the treating of life in a spirit of haste is so universal, Nietzsche speculates, is because everyone is in flight from himself or herself. Sometimes we do not wish to have the leisure to stop and think, for we might then be accosted by unpleasant memories that have a habit of suddenly asserting themselves (*Schopenhauer as Educator* 5). Nietzsche argues that we are, in fact, always in a condition where memories assail us, 'we live in fear of memory and of turning inward' because there 'are spirits all around us, every moment of our life wants to say something to us'. We have a real need, in fact, to deafen ourselves with sociability.

At issue for Nietzsche is our capacity for a critical or selective memory, what might be called a memory for life, that is attuned to its conditions of growth and flourishing. Both memory and forgetting enjoy an active mode of existence, as Nietzsche argues in this section, but both need also to be cultivated. They have a vital role to play in our becoming active, a becoming that takes place in the context of our encounters with various human sicknesses. Nietzsche stresses that forgetfulness is not something inert but an active ability to suppress without which there could be no mental order and equilibrium.[8] Without it we would be deprived of hope, pride, happiness and cheerfulness, and burdened with everything that has happened to us. Our head would become a noisy place, bustling with things we are unable to digest, and our actions would become paralysed. We would find ourselves unable to create anything new or even to be receptive to the arrival of the new. Nietzsche says that the person in whom this capacity has been damaged can be compared to a dyspeptic who cannot cope because they cannot finish with anything. Instead they engage in endless regurgitation and suffer from undigested experiences.

The person who becomes ill-constituted is someone who is plagued by memory traces that have been formed in the unconscious but which always invade consciousness. The problem is not simply that we are reactive as opposed to active in our existence, but that we don't act out our reactions. Instead, we come to feel our reactions and in this way open ourselves up to the poison of resentment. In the noble person, Nietzsche says, when resentment does take place it gets consumed and exhausted in some immediate reaction and, as a result, it does not poison. Our capacity for guilt and bad conscience is immense. When we become sick we enjoy being mistrustful, we dwell on wrongs and imagine all kinds of slights, we rummage through the bowels of our past for obscure, questionable stories which then allow us to wallow in tortured suspicion and to become intoxicated on our own poisonous wickedness; we will rip open old wounds and make ourselves bleed to death from scars long since healed, and friends, spouses and children all become the victims of our self-obsession (*On the Genealogy of Morality* III, 15). We seek to apportion blame for our suffering – something or someone or other must be to blame for our being so ill – and so become ripe for treatment by magicians of all kinds, including ascetic priests who know how to doctor us with balms and ointments but who poison the wound at the same time as tending to it.

For Nietzsche all of this makes us susceptible to misinterpretations: we are not reading the signs of life well, we are in fact misidentifying the causes of our suffering and feeling unwell, which are physiological. Nietzsche stresses, however, that he can hold to this view and yet still be a 'ferocious opponent of all materialism' (by which he must mean a scientific approach that would reduce everything to the level of a mechanical body). He holds that what constitutes health is a complex issue; any decision we make about the health of our body depends on several factors, including our powers and impulses, our goals and horizons, and what he calls 'the ideals and phantasms' of our soul (*The Gay Science* 120). Nietzsche is, in fact, opposed to the idea of there being something we can call 'health as such' and prefers to speak of there being innumerable healths of the body. Idealism in matters of living is something he also takes to task, not without good reason: 'Ignorance in *physiologis* – accursed "idealism" – is the real fatality in my life . . .' (*Ecce Homo* 'Why I am so clever' 2). His solution is to recommend selectivity in the things of life (nutriment, place and climate, recreation and so on) and the cultivation of taste as a very delicate art. To become what one is one must not have the slightest idea what one is; rather, one has to learn this: 'From this point of view the *blunders* of life . . . have their own meaning and value' (ibid. 9), including the wrong turnings we make, the delays of life, the holding back from things, the over-commitment to tasks that lie outside our capacity and so on. The events of a life are not to be read through the concepts of misfortune and guilt; one who knows how to forget can be 'strong enough for everything to *have* to turn out the best for him' (*Ecce Homo* 'Why I am so wise' 2).

For the frontispiece of his book *The Gay Science*, Nietzsche selected the following quotation from Emerson: 'All experiences are useful, all days are holy, and all human beings are divine.' He does not underestimate the testing nature of the attempt to live well. He knew this from first-hand experience, especially his relationship with Lou Salomé, which severely tested his alchemical approach to life, in which one endeavours to make gold out of the dung of one's experiences. As the relationship entered its last agonising throes, Nietzsche, in a letter to Franz Overbeck postmarked 25 December 1882, confessed to being broken on the wheel of his own passions. He has been suffering, he says, from humiliating and tormenting memories as from a bout of madness. This particular mouthful of life is the toughest one he has ever had to chew and one he might quite possibly choke on. At the same time, however, he writes to his friend, it provides him with the chance to prove what he seeks to preach – not only that all beings are divine, but also that the path to one's own heaven leads through the 'voluptuousness of one's own hell' (*The Gay Science* 338).

In speaking like this of our descent into a private hell, Nietzsche is not simply celebrating the perverse pleasure we can find in painful experiences, which was to become an important feature of Freud's attempt to comprehend what he identified as a morbid compulsion to repeat. Rather, Nietzsche develops this insight in the context of a critique of compassion. On the one hand, what we personally suffer from in life is incomprehensible and inaccessible to nearly everyone else. The feeling of compassion strips suffering of its personal character, to the point where, Nietzsche says, our so-called benefactors diminish our worth and will more than our enemies do. On the other hand, those who are keen to demonstrate compassion fail to comprehend the formative character of our suffering and the fact that we are capable of finding the resources to learn and profit from it. They do not understand that there is a 'personal necessity' in misfortune in which the deprivations, impoverishments, adventures, risks and blunders are as necessary to us as the opposite. The fact that vital parts of the economy of one's being are involved in one's misfortunes, such as the breaking open of new springs and needs, the healing of old wounds, and the shedding of entire periods of one's past, do not concern the compassionate person.

6

LIFE IS A WOMAN, OR THE ULTIMATE BEAUTIES

Vita femina. – Not even all knowledge and all good will suffice for seeing the ultimate beauties of a work; it requires the rarest of lucky accidents for the clouds that veil the peaks to lift for us momentarily and for the sun to shine on them. Not only must we stand in just the right spot to see this, but our own soul, too, must itself have pulled the veil from its heights and must have been in need of some external expression and parable, as if it needed a hold in order to retain control of itself. But so rarely does all of this coincide that I am inclined to believe that the highest peaks of everything good, be it work, deed, humanity, or nature, have so far remained hidden and covered from the majority and even from the best. But what does unveil itself for us *unveils itself for us only once*! The Greeks, to be sure, prayed: 'Everything beautiful twice and thrice!' Indeed, they had good reason to summon the gods, for ungodly reality gives us the beautiful either never or only once! I mean to say that the world is brimming with beautiful things but nevertheless poor, very poor in beautiful moments and in the unveilings of those things. But perhaps that is the strongest magic of life: it is covered by a veil of beautiful possibilities, woven with threads of gold – promising, resisting, bashful, mocking, compassionate, and seductive. Yes, life is a woman!

Extract from *The Gay Science*, aphorism 339

This intriguing aphorism, taken from the concluding series of aphorisms of book four of *The Gay Science*, contains a number of enigmatic aspects. The aphorism is pertinent to the reading of Nietzsche I have been pursuing in the last two chapters since it indicates that there is something in our experience of life that lies outside incorporation, namely, the highest peaks and the most beautiful moments (we shall encounter the issue of incorporation again in the next chapter). It resonates with other aphorisms in book four and with others encountered in the preceding three books of the text, especially book two. In previous aphorisms in book four Nietzsche has signalled on more than one occasion the importance of developing a genuine knowledge of things and of ourselves. For example, he has reflected upon: the 'severity of science', which demands we take up residence in a 'masculine' air (293); the importance of making our experiences a matter of conscience for our knowledge, which involves practising a type of honesty that is alien to all founders of religion and to moral systems (319); approaching life as an experiment for the knowledge-seeker, which is to be treated not as a duty, a disaster or a deception; and employing physics (methods of observation and self-observation) in the service of self-legislation and self-creation (335). In this aphorism, however, Nietzsche is drawing our attention to the significance of an aspect of our experience of life which lies outside the efforts of knowledge: the unveiling of the ultimate beauties.

The extent to which it is problematic for Nietzsche to construe issues of knowledge and life by relying on gender stereotypes, which is not specific to this aphorism, is an issue that must inevitably be raised. I do not think that the insight he is offering in this aphorism is completely determined by his figuration of woman, nor do I think there is anything sexist in his claim that 'life is a woman'. I will offer my reading of the aphorism and then leave the reader to decide on the issue.

The claim made at the end of the aphorism that 'life is a

woman' is not difficult to decipher: life is a seduction and a temptation and for this reason can be compared to 'woman' (the beloved object). Moreover, life is a woman in the sense in which one loves life and loves another in terms of a possible world, one that promises and that lures. As such a world it can resist us, appear bashful, mock our efforts, show compassion towards us and so on. What is much more difficult to decipher is Nietzsche's claim in the main part of the aphorism that 'what does unveil itself for us *unveils itself for us only once*!' Just what is this unveiling? And why, with regard to each thing that is unveiled, does it take place only once? It is difficult to determine exactly why Nietzsche holds the view he does and he does not give us any reasons for it in the aphorism. We have to bring the art of interpretation to bear on it and this requires paying close attention to his words and opening up the movements of thought at work in it.

The first key point Nietzsche makes in the aphorism, which should compel our attention, is that seeing the ultimate beauties of a work is not dependent upon either our knowledge or the possession of a good will. He stresses that only the rarest of lucky accidents can bring such seeing about. We need to be standing in the right spot and our own soul must also have pulled the veil from its heights. In this double unveiling what is taking place is not some correspondence between an inside and an outside, such as a physical peak and an internal psychic height, but simply the seeing of the beautiful in an especially intensive manner; it is what we might call seeing beyond intention. This is to speak of the desire of our seeing and the innocence of this seeing. Nietzsche says that it is rare for all of this to coincide, which explains why the highest peaks of everything good have hitherto remained hidden not only from the majority but from the best, too. For the most part we do not see the beautiful things that populate the world. These are always there but are concealed from us because of our immersion in the habits of life and life's givenness (it's always going to be here and we are always going to be here). It is a fact of our existence that the world is poor in beautiful moments and the unveiling of the ultimate beauties. We are creatures of sense and meaning who dwell in a universe devoid of sense and meaning (this is the 'ungodly reality' named in the aphorism). Imagine seeing the ultimate beauties all the time. They would not be ultimate beauties. Rather, they are the beauties one sees at singular, rare and precarious moments of life and that have no objective existence independent of such moments. They do not disclose to us anything about the world, but are bound up with the desire of our seeing. Although an ecstatic human life is one that turns on the seeing of these ultimate beauties, Nietzsche is not advocating that we lead such a life (this seeing cannot be willed). The only life that can be advocated for Nietzsche is one that carries with it the 'heaviest weight' and for him this can be just as inspirational; in fact, more deeply so.

Nietzsche has already touched upon the subject matter of this aphorism in an earlier text, *Human, All Too Human*. In aphorism 586, entitled 'Of the hour-hand of life', he writes that life 'consists of rare individual moments of the highest significance and countless intervals in which at best the phantoms of those moments hover about us'. He goes on to state that 'love, spring, a beautiful melody, the mountains, the moon, the sea', speak to our heart only once, 'if they do in fact truly find speech'. This helps to decipher the aphorism I have selected from *The Gay Science*. The highest moments or peaks of life are ones that stand out from the flow of time and the regular course of things; they are sufficient in themselves and do not require incorporation. Certain forms and expressions of language seek to convey the experience of this perception: the poet and the writer of parables, for example (as in Nietzsche's narration of the highest peaks of Zarathustra). The countless intervals are precisely the ones that belong to the regular form of time and that serve to mark and calculate time's passing (the monotonous beats of a life); in the beautiful moments, by contrast, there is only the one time that is the mark of a singular insight or perception. This is the ultimate beauty, which is ultimate because we will see it only once. Like the hour-hand of a clock these moments are few and far between in contrast to the minutes that tick away. Something of this informs Nietzsche's decision to write (to mark) the once or one time as *Ein Mal*. He splits the word in two when he could have used the normal expression *einmal* (as he does in *Human, All Too Human* 586). *Mal* names not only time but also sign, mark, monument, stigma and birthmark; in short, it names something that stands out and indicates a certain ecstasy of being that is decisive for us, rendering our lives vital and eventful.

We can speak of the unveiling of the highest peaks of everything good as enjoying a singular existence – it does not belong to a numerical order or multiplicity – because it is a revelation that stands out from everything we have hitherto known and perceived (through a veil) and everything we will subsequently encounter. Life appears worth living in such moments and possesses a special intensity. However, the experience of the highest peaks brings with it certain dangers. We can spend the greatest portion of our lives living in their shadow because we think that they have afforded us moments of supreme perception. This judgement is a perilous one since it involves giving too much weight and significance to what is, ultimately, a beautiful illusion or appearance.

Nietzsche's aphorism is not lamenting the veiling and inviting us to see without veils. Neither does the unveiling refer to seeing things as they really are since this makes no sense in Nietzsche's thinking (we see things only under the perspectival conditions of our affects or emotions). Rather, it is an experience of seeing things in a way that differs from our habitual modes. Nietzsche is not advocating a contemplative life or suggesting that we remove ourselves from the world in order to have only the enjoyment of the highest peaks (they cannot be willed). Even our contemplative power belies a creative power and we are always the poets and authors of our lives. We are never simply contemplating the world but always creating it (*The Gay Science* 301). Human beings are distinguished from animals by the fact that they see and hear more, and higher human beings distinguish themselves from lower ones by thoughtfully seeing and hearing immeasurably more. On account of this thoughtfulness a higher human being becomes happier and unhappier at the same time. However, such a human being gets caught under the spell of a delusion when they suppose that they are placed before the visual and acoustic play of life as a spectator and listener. It is we who have created the world that concerns us as human beings. This is a knowledge we lack, and when we do grasp it for a moment we forget it the next. Nietzsche ends the aphorism by saying that we are neither as proud nor as happy as we might be.

In this aphorism on *Vita femina* Nietzsche is drawing our attention to an element in our knowing and willing which lies outside our powers of incorporation. This is the element of chance and the lucky accident. In *Thus Spoke Zarathustra* Nietzsche institutes chance as a key concept in his thinking beyond good and evil, naming 'Lord Chance' as the world's oldest nobility which liberates things from purpose and its servitude. There is only a heaven or sky of chance, of innocence, of accident and of wantonness (*Thus Spoke Zarathustra*

'Before Sunrise'). This is the chance that we do endeavour to incorporate and in terms of the love of fate that informs our projects and plans. The movement of thought in this aphorism is not one from a tone of lamentation to one of consolation and ultimately affirmation; it is affirmative from beginning to end. Nietzsche is drawing attention to the different forms of time that characterise and punctuate a life (the different truths of time). Life has its singular and supreme moments but, at the same time, it is to be lived in the only way we can live it, namely as 'covered by a veil of beautiful possibilities'. Moreover, life cannot be lived as a beautiful dream but demands the *work* of love. Life can be effectively and truly lived only by dwelling in the space and time of its imposing realities. The seeing of an ultimate beauty cannot return (it takes place, recall, only once); but the demands of existence come back to us again and again.

Aphorism 277 contains some wise advice concerning all of this. It begins by referring to a certain high point in life which, once reached, grants us a certain freedom but also signals, paradoxically, that we now face the great danger of spiritual unfreedom. This is because, although we have confronted the beautiful chaos of existence, and so denied the existence of any and all providential reason, we still have to pass our hardest test. This consists in knowing just what it means to incorporate fate and love it. The risk we run is that of falling prey to the error of placing meaning where it does not belong (in reality). This will lead us astray by making us believe that mystical forces are at work in our lives, such as the divinatory powers of gods and genies. Isn't it extraordinary how every day and every hour life seems to want to prove to us the proposition that everything that befalls us turns out for the best, be it the weather, the loss of a friend, a sickness, a letter that fails to arrive, a dream, the opening of a book and so on? All this shows, Nietzsche argues, is that our own skill in interpreting and arranging the events that happen to us has reached an apex.

There are several aphorisms in book two of *The Gay Science* that can serve to expand our comprehension of Nietzsche's lesson in aphorism 339. It begins with an aphorism entitled 'To the realists' (57) that takes to task those he calls 'the sober realists' who hold themselves to be well-armed against passion and phantastical conceptions and wish to make their emptiness an issue of pride and ornament. These unmagical realists, as they might be called, want to believe that the way the world appears to them is the way it really is and that before them reality stands unveiled. These realists are, in fact, ignorant of the event of unveiling and do not understand the nature of unveiling (they do not understand what is being unveiled). But this love of reality, Nietzsche says, remains a love and an ancient one at that, carrying with it the valuations of things that originated in the passions and loves of former centuries. Every object we focus our perception on, be it a cloud in the sky or a mountain in the distance, contains an element of phantasy and of fear, prejudice, ignorance and so on. The realists who seek to subtract the phantasm from the real simply wish to escape from the intoxication of knowing and perceiving. Perhaps these realists are 'altogether *incapable* of drunkenness'. Book two ends with Nietzsche expressing an ultimate gratitude to art because it displays 'the good will to appearance' (107). Art 'furnishes us with the eye and the hand and above all the good conscience to be *able* to make . . . a phenomenon of ourselves'. It enables us to locate the hero as well as the fool in our passion for knowledge, giving us the means and the extended power to look at and down upon ourselves from an artistic distance. We need our folly, though, in order to pursue the wisdom of our knowledge and we need it against ourselves and our grave nature: 'we need all exuberant, floating, dancing, mocking, childish, and blissful art' precisely in order not to lose 'that *freedom over things* that our ideal demands of us' (see also 299). The theme of art and the real is continued in the ensuing aphorisms (58–60) and aphorism 60 on 'women and their action at a distance' can be read productively alongside 339. In book four, aphorism 299 is devoted to the topic of 'what we should learn from artists'. In it Nietzsche discusses the means we have for making things beautiful, attractive and desirable even when they are not. The beautiful is an artistic construction and fabrication, involving distance, the multiplication of perspectives, and giving things a surface and skin that is not fully transparent.

This final book of the original edition of *The Gay Science* is devoted in large part to the topic of the role played in life by chance and accident and is a meditation on the beautiful. It begins with Nietzsche declaring 'for the new year' what shall be his love from now on, which he states to be *amor fati* or the love of (one's) fate. He states that he wishes to stop waging war on the ugly and to distance himself from any image of torment (literally a 'martyr-image' in the German). His ambition, he says, 'would find no satisfaction if I wanted to make myself a sublime torturer' (313; in *Thus Spoke Zarathustra* he speaks of the need to become an exalted human being (*Gehobener*) and not merely a sublime one (*Erhabener*)). The opening aphorism of *The Gay Science* finds him stating that he wishes 'to learn more and more how to see what is necessary in things as what is beautiful in them', and in this way be someone who makes things beautiful (276). He wants only to be a 'yea-sayer'. This is what is captured in the formula *amor fati*.

Traditionally, as in the tragedies of ancient Greece for example, fate refers to the world of fortune that lies beyond human control or influence. The love of fate that Nietzsche speaks of involves learning what it means to live in the element of chance and accident. It's not a matter of looking for any deep meaning to what happens to us, but rather simply a matter of living life in terms of artistic transfiguration and knowing that we are doing this (see also *The Gay Science* 290). We can then be honest with ourselves about our fantasies and projections and see them for the constructions they are.

Concerning the analogy Nietzsche makes between woman and art and appearance, one commentator has argued that this is not to trivialise women, as has often been suggested, since he is taking male fantasies about women to provide the paradigm cases of projections that are taken to be objectively true. Nietzsche's exploration of art and reality serves to remind the reader that these fantasies are neither objectively true nor an approximation of women's own perspectives. His thinking involves the strategy of reminding us that perspectives are not fixed and that perspectivism is an activity, one in which his own readers are forced to participate.[9]

What is the 'only once' and why 'only once'? If the seeing of an ultimate beauty is not something we can will into existence then it is impossible for us to will that it come back; the lucky accident that brings it about lies outside the exertion of the will. With regard to the second question we can take note of what Nietzsche says about the Greeks praying for 'everything beautiful twice and thrice!' and that they had good reason to summon their gods since an ungodly reality gives us it either never or only once. But this doesn't solve the riddle of why he thinks the unveiling of some ultimate beauty happens for us only once (it is obviously interesting that Nietzsche thinks that mature, modern human beings who dwell in an ungodly reality are fully able to live life on the level of beautiful possibilities). An answer to the riddle is that the moment of oneness which characterises the seeing of an ultimate beauty, in which a double unveiling takes place that dissolves distances and boundaries, is necessarily an instance and instant of erasure and obliteration, one that appears like lightning. It's impossible for consciousness to assimilate or incorporate this experience; it can, therefore, only ever be an experience of the 'only once' – even if it happens again. It is a moment of bliss and oblivion.

In later writings Nietzsche clarifies and refines what it means to say 'yes' to life: it doesn't mean that one says yes to everything and it doesn't exclude the 'no'. Living life in terms of its beautiful possibilities does not mean we cannot recognise what is ugly and face what strikes us as terrifying and intolerable; rather, our task is to aim to be equal to everything that happens in life, the great and the small, the highest and the lowest. As Nietzsche appreciated, there is something sublime in this (something of the realm of the unknown), and in aspiring to be equal to life we necessarily have to appeal to what is sublime in us.

7

THE HEAVIEST WEIGHT

The heaviest weight. – What if some day or night a demon were to steal into your loneliest loneliness and say to you: 'This life as you now live it and have lived it you will have to live once again and innumerable times again; and there will be nothing new in it, but every pain and every joy and every thought and sigh and everything unspeakably small or great in your life must return to you, all in the same succession and sequence – even this spider and this moonlight between the trees, and even this moment and I myself. The eternal hourglass of existence is turned over again and again, and you with it, speck of dust!' Would you not throw yourself down and gnash your teeth and curse the demon who spoke thus? Or have you once experienced a tremendous moment when you would have answered him: 'You are a god, and never have I heard anything more divine.' If this thought gained power over you, as you are it would transform and possibly crush you; the question in each and every thing, 'Do you want this again and innumerable times again?' would lie on your actions as the heaviest weight! Or how well disposed would you have to become to yourself and to life *to long for nothing more fervently* than for this ultimate eternal confirmation and seal?

Extract from *The Gay Science*, aphorism 341

This is the penultimate aphorism of the fourth and final book of the original edition of *The Gay Science*. It is sandwiched between an aphorism on the last words of Socrates ('the dying Socrates') and one on 'the tragedy begins', where the figure of Zarathustra is first introduced in Nietzsche's writings. *The Gay Science* 341 is Nietzsche's first published presentation of the thought of the eternal return or recurrence of the same (later presentations can be found in *Thus Spoke Zarathustra* 'Of the Vision and the Riddle' and 'The Convalescent', *Beyond Good and Evil* 56, and *Twilight of the Idols* 'What I Owe to the Ancients', 4 and 5).[10] In order to gain a proper appreciation of the expectations Nietzsche had for the thought, and the concerns that led him to it, we need to examine the original sketches of the thought he composed in the summer of 1881. Nietzsche conceived eternal return as offering the highest formula of the affirmation of life attainable, and it is a thought that has had a wide-ranging influence on modern consciousness. It has been taken up by philosophers as different as Stanley Cavell and Gilles Deleuze, it has found its way into novels, such as Milan Kundera's *The Unbearable Lightness of Being*, and it has inspired several works of cinema from the populist *Groundhog Day* to Andrei Tarkovsky's masterpiece *Sacrifice*.

In some of his notebooks Nietzsche sought to come up with a cosmological proof for the thought and even to link it up with the laws of the relatively new science of thermo-dynamics. The cosmological aspect of the thought, however, has failed to satisfy commentators and it is difficult to imagine that a credible physics could be found that would lend support to it. In its initial formulation in 1881–2 Nietzsche conceived it not as a new theory of the world but as a new teaching. In a note from 1881 he writes that although the circular repetition of things might be only a probability or possibility, the thought of a possibility can still shatter and transform us, and he invites us to consider how the possibility of eternal damnation has worked. In its initial articulation eternal return is

Nietzsche's response to the set of problems that he has worked through in his free-spirit period of 1878–82, notably the death of God. He speaks of our having lost the centre of gravity – the heaviest weight – that allowed us to live, and now we are unsure how to get in or out of life. The old teaching offered by the Christian-moral hypothesis placed the centre of gravity outside life, in a beyond and an otherworldly God. The new teaching of eternal return seeks to provide a new centre of gravity focused on the immanent conditions and form of a life. Our desire to get out of life should be one that enables us to attain an exalted perspective on it and has the effect of returning us to our actual life in a more profound and committed way. The affirmation of life centres on the task of being equal to it with respect to all its aspects and in the face of the sternest and strangest problems it throws up for us.

Hitherto religion has taught human beings to despise this life as merely transitory and to cast their hopes on an indeterminate other life. For Nietzsche, however, we cannot now rest content with a shallow atheism which encourages us to devote all our energies of knowledge and being to a fleeting life (what energy is required for this?). Rather, the task, he says, is to impress the likeness of eternity on this life as the only life we shall ever have. In one of the sketches from 1881 Nietzsche presents eternal return as a critique of the political delusion of secularisation which seeks only the well-being of the transient individual. The fruit of this process, he says, is socialism, in which transient individuals desire only to encompass their happiness through material comfort and an easy life, or what he calls 'socialisation'. In short, secularisation avoids the need to think about life and refrains from making intellectual demands on human beings. In contrast to this Nietzsche offers a teaching which says that the task is to live one's life in such a way that one wants it again, and to do this it is necessary to find out what gives one the highest feeling.[11] In the published presentation in *The Gay Science* 341 this is set out in terms of our becoming well disposed towards ourselves and life. It is clear that Nietzsche feared that a widespread state of apathy and indifference towards life would emerge in the wake of God's death. The thought of eternal return is designed to combat this.

Eternal return parodies the idea of an ultimate selection, one that would come at the end of one's life as a final judgement and determine whether one goes to heaven or to hell. In offering the heaviest weight Nietzsche parodies imagery borrowed from the Zoroastrian religion for the attainment of heaven, which can take place only through the test of ethical achievement. The fate of each individual is decided at a bridge that hangs over an abyss. At the bridge an individual's thoughts and deeds from the age of fifteen onwards are weighed against one another. If those that accord with goodness weigh heavier then the individual is granted access to the great, luminous mansion in the sky; those in whom evil thoughts and deeds weigh heavier are condemned to the netherworld or hell. Nietzsche's thought makes no appeal to a judgement of goodness conceived as a transcendent or metaphysical standard. Only we ourselves can make a selection of what is important and significant in our lives, and the thought of eternal return seeks to give us a means to do this. It does not condemn us to an infinitely repeated life in which we are powerless to transform ourselves and our lives, but asks us to incorporate in our lives as a musical refrain the following question: do I want this again and again? In this way we can gain a sense of the weight of the things we do and desire to do.

Eternal return is a thought that promises not the advent of a better life or an afterlife, but rather the return of an identical life. The 'same' refers to the temporal conditions and form of our earthly life. There is no escape from this and no salvation. The thought comes at a critical hour of life, confronts us with our ultimate insignificance (we specks of dust) and offers no final consolation. The thought will transform us and even knock us out. The title of this aphorism in German is literally 'the greatest heavyweight', and Nietzsche intends the boxing reference. Even if one wishes to consider seriously the teaching in its cosmological aspect, it is important to appreciate that the recurrences of a life would take place in terms that are qualitatively identical and differ only on a numerical level. There would be, then, no real difference between living life once and living it innumerable times; it is the same life that we always live and return to. We always come back to life and return to its conditions (this moonlight), repeating the tasks of incorporation, and transforming all that we are into light and flame (like the spider that weaves).

Nietzsche's first sketch of the eternal return is dated 'early August 1881, Sils-Maria' and signed '6,000 feet above sea level and higher than all human things'. It is a sketch for a book in five parts on the return of the same. The main theme is incorporation, showing that Nietzsche's initial focus was on how human beings could come to live the thought and make use of it. The first part will be on the incorporation of the fundamental errors; the second on the incorporation of the passions; the third on the incorporation of knowledge in terms of the passion of knowledge; the fourth is on 'the innocent', 'the individual as experiment' and 'the easing of life'; while the fifth and final part will present the doctrine as the new burden and address the 'infinite importance of our knowing, our erring, of our habits and modes of life for everything to come'. The question is posed: 'What shall we do with the *rest* of our lives – we who have spent them for the most part in the most profound ignorance?' The answer given is that the greatest teaching, to be offered as our kind of blessedness, will be taught as the most powerful means of incorporating it into ourselves. Nietzsche says we must 'wait and see how far *knowledge* and *truth* can be *incorporated*' in order to determine what new habits of living are required from us as beings who now live largely in order to know. The question is then posed: 'What will life look like from the point of view of its sum total of well-being?' The sketch concludes by appealing to the principle of indifference (which must have worked its way deep inside us) and asks 'whether we still *want to live*: and how!'[12] What we are indifferent to are the first and last things of metaphysics, not our actual lives. The task before us is that of no longer living in ignorance of ourselves and to stop leading an imaginary existence or a merely ephemeral one.

In *The Gay Science* 341 Nietzsche has chosen a particular form of address as a way of communicating the thought. The words come from the strange voice of a demon who 'steals' into our life at a particular hour, that of our loneliest loneliness, and speaks to us as specks of dust. Traditionally the voice of the demon represents that of fear and doubt, even terror. Perhaps the strongest connection to be made is with Socrates' demon. The Greek term *daimon* means divider or allotter, and from Homer onwards it refers to the operator of unanticipated and intrusive events in life; the adjective *daimonios* means strange and uncanny. Later the word came also to acquire the meaning of a guardian or protector, a spirit who accompanies a person's life and brings them either luck or misfortune. In Plato the *daimon* operates as an intermediary between god and human beings and this conception was taken up by all subsequent demonologies. Socrates spoke of his demon in terms of being subject to a divine or supernatural experience in which a voice comes to him to dissuade him from what he is proposing to do. In Nietzsche's aphorism the words of the demon are designed neither to persuade nor dissuade; rather, they give us the means to find out something essential concerning our disposition towards life and the things we desire to will.

It has been suggested by some commentators that Nietzsche conceived eternal return working as a kind of deathbed revelation in which the loneliest loneliness refers to the actual hour of one's death (the fact that this aphorism on the eternal return comes after one on the last words of Socrates gives good grounds for this interpretation). Would we be able at the end of our life to look back and affirm everything great and small that has taken place in it, to the point where we would want it again and would be willing to live it in exactly the same sequence? How well disposed towards life would we have to be to say yes to this? Or would our desire express itself in the wish to escape from life and be relieved of it? I think this offers too literal a reading of the hour of our loneliest loneliness (the aphorism opens by simply speaking of 'some day or night'). I take it to refer to the time when we are caught at our lowest ebb, the hardest time of life when we are perhaps looking for consolation and salvation and yet are honest enough with ourselves to acknowledge that none will be forthcoming. Nietzsche selects this time so as to present us with the ultimate challenge conceivable, and without pity or compassion. The thought of eternal return will, ultimately, transform and maybe crush us (it could make us despair of life even more); or perhaps the thought will inspire us to become so well disposed towards ourselves and life that we want nothing more ardently than the ultimate eternal confirmation and seal offered by it. The thought is clearly working as a thought-experiment that makes no truth-claims. Thus, any suppositions about its cosmological status are irrelevant.

A number of aphorisms in book four of *The Gay Science* address the different kinds of voices that speak to us. *The Gay Science* 278, for example, speaks of the 'melancholy happiness' we experience from living in a jumble of lanes, needs and voices. For Nietzsche the task is to hear the right kinds of voices, for example, to hear the voice of the intellectual conscience over the moral one (*The Gay Science* 335), and to train one's reason so as not to experience miracles and rebirths or hear the voices of angels (*The Gay Science* 319). Unlike that of an angel, the demon's voice is not one that seeks to comfort or console. It is the voice of our higher and nobler self, the voice that inspires us to practise the unity of life and thought and that makes extraordinary demands on us that challenge any tendency we might have to intellectual cowardice or moral laziness.

There are two quite different aspects to Nietzsche's presentation in *The Gay Science* 341, a fact that is often overlooked in commentaries which tend to focus only on the first part of the aphorism. In it a demon tells us that the life we have lived we shall have to live not just once more but innumerable times more with nothing new in it, and everything, however small or great, that has marked it will come back to us in the same sequence. We are then asked to consider in the aphorism's second part how we would respond. We might suppose that Nietzsche's thought-experiment has a nasty and cruel side to it since it seems to impose a quite dreadful curse. To perceive the promise of the thought, however, two things need to come into view. First, have we once experienced a moment so tremendous that it would be possible for us to greet the thought as a divine one worthy of being affirmed? The promise of the return of such a moment is one that might inspire us to affirm the thought and all that it entails (affirming the small as well as the great). Second, there is the quite different issue of the thought gaining power over us and for this we need to want to discover ourselves and become the ones that we are. Supposing it did, a peculiar kind of question in each and every thing would come to lie upon our actions as the heaviest weight.

This second aspect of the presentation is crucial and should not be overlooked. As a practical synthesis eternal return can intervene in our lives and play a supervening role on all our other thoughts. In a sketch from 1881, for example, which is an outline for what became the second part of *The Gay Science* 341, Nietzsche presents it as the 'thought of thoughts' and offers it as a response to a well-known philosophical problem: to what extent are we free in what we do or is everything predetermined? Nietzsche expresses it as a task of gaining a degree of power over our actions: 'Thought and belief are a weight pressing down on me as much as and even more than any other weight. You say that food, a location, air, society transform and condition you: well your opinions do so even more, since it is they that determine your choice of food, dwelling, air, society. If you incorporate this thought within you, amongst your other thoughts, it will transform you. The question in everything that you will: "am I certain I want to do it an infinite number of times?" will become for you the heaviest weight.'[13] In other words, although we are nothing other than an accumulation of habits and memories that have been passively contracted, it is possible for us to become the ones that we are by constituting ourselves as agents of life, as opposed to being simply patients of it. The thought doesn't tell us what our 'good' is but simply gives us the means to discover it and put it to the test, and in this way we become those that we are: 'the ones who are new, unique, incomparable, the self-legislating, the self-creating' (*The Gay Science* 335).

Nietzsche's practical rule offers a new centre of gravity as we endeavour to become well disposed towards ourselves and life. Becoming the ones that we are, however, is not a simple matter of moral conscience but requires the stern application of conscientious knowledge (he speaks of the intellectual conscience working as a conscience behind our conscience, which is to name the superior form of conscience). In previous aphorisms of book four Nietzsche has written in praise of the virtue of honesty or probity and of the need for us to become our own experiments and guinea pigs (*The Gay Science* 319 and 335). Nietzsche is not offering self-creation as a fantasy but as a task (two aphorisms in book four speak of the value of doing something 'again and again', *The Gay Science* 304 and 334).

With the thought of eternal return Nietzsche is inviting us to unlearn the metaphysical universe so that we direct our energies on what is closest to us. It would be absurd to take it as offering a 'solution' to the problem of life. It necessarily has its limits and is a thought to be experimented with – creatively and conscientiously.

8

THE SUPERMAN

There it was too that I picked up the word 'Superman' and that man is something that must be overcome,

that man is a bridge and not a goal; counting himself happy for his noontides and evenings, as a way to new dawns:

Zarathustra's saying of the great noontide, and whatever else I have hung up over men, like a purple evening afterglow.

Truly, I showed them new stars, together with new nights – and over cloud and day and night I spread out laughter like a coloured canopy.

I taught them all *my* art and aims: to compose into one and bring together what is fragment and riddle and dreadful chance in man –

as poet, reader of riddles, and redeemer of chance, I taught them to create the future, and to redeem by creating – all that *was past*.

To redeem that past of mankind and to transform every 'It was', until the will says: 'But I willed it thus! So shall I will it –'

this did I call redemption, this alone did I teach them to call redemption.

Now I await *my* redemption – that I may go to them for the last time.

For I want to go to man once more: I want to go under *among* them, I want to give them, dying, my richest gift!

From the sun when it goes down, that superabundant star, I learned this: then, from inexhaustible riches it pours out gold into the sea –

so that the poorest fisherman rows with *golden* oars! For once I
saw this, and did not tire of weeping to see it.

Like the sun, Zarathustra also wants to go down: now he sits here
and waits, old shattered law-tables around him and also new law-
tables – half-written.

Extract from *Thus Spoke Zarathustra*,
'Of Old and New Law-Tables', section 3

In *The Gay Science* 342, the final aphorism of the original
edition of the book, Nietzsche introduces the figure of
Zarathustra. He draws upon this aphorism to stage the opening of *Thus Spoke Zarathustra*. After ten years enjoying his
spirit and solitude in the mountains Zarathustra has become
sick of his wisdom, like a bee that has collected too much
honey, and now desires outstretched hands into which he can
give it away. He makes the decision to descend and 'become
human again'. He will teach human beings that the earth is in
need of a new meaning and direction.

This introduces us to Nietzsche's idea of the superman,
which has often been the subject of wild caricature. It was
used by Nazi ideologues to promote and justify the cause of a
pure, Aryan 'master race'. It is important to note that racial
fantasies play no part in Nietzsche's thinking. However, as we
shall see in the next chapter, he does have fantasies of his
own, including fantasies about the superman. The significance of the notion has been interpreted in different ways by
Nietzsche's philosophical commentators and readers. For
Gilles Deleuze it denotes a new sense and sensibility of the
human grounded in a vision and riddle of a new earth and
new people to come. Other thinkers, such as Martin
Heidegger (1889–1976), have sought to render the idea pertinent to the ecological and planetary crisis of the modern age.

In *Thus Spoke Zarathustra* the superman is offered as a
noble ideal of self-overcoming, which involves the self

freely exploring the heights and abysses of its existence as a mortal creature of the earth. Getting the precise measure of the notion is not easy; indeed, it was designed by him to test the measure of man. On the one hand, Nietzsche has Zarathustra stress the importance of placing the energies of our knowledge on what is humanly conceivable and humanly palpable (*Thus Spoke Zarathustra* 'On the Blissful Islands'). Zarathustra invites us to consider the following question: can we conceive a god as that which is perfect, unmoved and permanent? Whenever we try to do so we always come up with a thought that makes all that is straight crooked and all that stands giddy. Time suddenly disappears, since it is declared to be unreal, and all that is transitory is said to be a lie. In the effort to conceive such a being our mind experiences vertigo and our stomach feels sick. We have a problem of digestion. On the other hand, however, he urges us to become more and other than human. The difficulty lies in determining the precise sense of this more.

In the prologue to the book Zarathustra descends to the market-place and declares: 'The Superman shall now be the meaning of the earth.' To the people Zarathustra speaks of the most contemptible human being, which is the type he designates as 'the last man'. This is the man who no longer wishes to pose questions of existence but is content with his lot on earth. The modern discovery of happiness as the solution to the problem of human existence provides him with the answer he needs. Zarathustra however, is a severe taskmaster who teaches that what is great about man is that he is a bridge and not a goal. The task of human existence is to become more than human. The human is 'fragment, riddle, and dreadful chance'; it is material to be worked upon. The superman can only be the project of an experiment.

Nietzsche wants us to conquer two things: our metaphysical needs and the animal certitudes of our existence.

In *Ecce Homo* Nietzsche tells his readers that *Thus Spoke Zarathustra* was written under unfavourable, even improbable, circumstances. He is referring to the depression he experienced in the wake of the collapse of his friendship with Rée and Salomé. Nietzsche emerged from it with newfound philosophical riches. *Thus Spoke Zarathustra* offers nothing less than a new kind of philosophical practice conceived as the art of transfiguration, in which a multiplicity of states and modes of being is treated and traversed, including states of intoxication, dream, sleep, awakening, and states of indecision and decision. In *Ecce Homo* Nietzsche calls Zarathustra a type, the physiological presupposition of which is 'great health'. This is a cheerful health, strong, shrewd, tough and daring, that will belong to the new and nameless ones of a 'premature-born yet undemonstrated future'. Nietzsche outlines the nature of this health in aphorism 382 of book five of *The Gay Science* written in 1887, and he quotes from it in his discussion of Zarathustra in *Ecce Homo*. It is not a health that one can say one simply possesses, because one has to continually win it and sacrifice it again and again. It is a dangerous health for this reason and involves a law of repetition, a testing of the boundaries of a land 'beyond all known lands' and one that is overfull with the beautiful, the strange, the questionable and the terrible.

Such a type is captivated by an ideal of a new kind of spirit, one that plays impulsively and from overflowing plenitude and power with all that has hitherto been called good, holy and untouchable (the secrets of life perhaps). And yet, for all the emphasis placed on the playful disposition of this type Nietzsche is also able to speak of the great seriousness arising for the first time with the advent of this new being, 'the real question-mark is first set up . . . the tragedy *begins* . . .' (*Ecce Homo*, '*Thus Spoke Zarathustra*', section 2). The task is not, however, simply one of converting people to this type, 'because we do not easily admit that anyone has a *right to it*'. Zarathustra is a dancer and musician of life, one who has undergone the most fearful insight into reality and experienced the most abysmal thought (the eternal return of life) and finds in them no objection to existence, but rather 'one more reason *to be himself* the eternal Yes to all things', able to declare: '"Into every abyss I still bear the blessing of my affirmation"' (ibid., section 6). This is not the affirmation that does not know how to say no and which belongs to the ass that chews and digests everything it comes across, saying yea to everything.

The Iranian prophet Zarathustra, 'he who can manage camels', known more generally under the later Greek form of Zoroaster, saw existence as the eventual realisation of a divine plan and foretold of its fulfilment when everything would be made perfect once and for all. The cosmos does not simply exist but has a purpose to it. The universe is depicted by the ancient prophet in profoundly moral terms, conceived as a struggle between two spirits embodied in forces that maintain the cosmos and those that strive to undermine it. These are the forces of good and evil, of creation and destruction (*asha* and *druj*). The divine plan foretells a time when the 'lie' of the spirit of destruction and active evil will be destroyed and the creative good will prevail everywhere. The cosmos will then be rid of the forces of chaos once and for all. This will, in fact, mark the end of the limited time which has so far contained the cosmos and the beginning of a reign of a blissful eternity. A great separation will take place in contrast to the time of mixture that has hitherto ruled.

It seems certain that Nietzsche was familiar with the details of the Zoroastrian religion, including its sacred scriptures known as the *Avesta* ('authoritative utterance'). There are many allusions to these details, and parodies of them, running throughout the book. The fact that Zarathustra may have meant he who manages camels is an important reference for understanding the significance of Nietzsche's depiction of the metamorphoses his Zarathustra must undergo, transforming the heavy weightiness of existence into something that can be endured and made light and free (the opening discourse of the work is entitled 'The Three Metamorphoses', which refer to the camel, the lion and the child). It is only in *Ecce Homo* that Nietzsche discloses the reason why he has chosen the name of the ancient Persian prophet Zarathustra. Because Zarathustra created the most fateful of errors – morality and its translation into the realm of metaphysics – he must be the first to recognise it. It is for this reason that Nietzsche construes the task as one of morality overcoming itself through truthfulness, the latter being the supreme virtue upheld by the ancient prophet. It is now time to rid the world of the metaphysics of good and evil. This will constitute a new truth and a new virtue, naming the self-overcoming of morality which has to become flesh in us. This self-overcoming does not mean the end or cancellation of morality but represents a conquest in our knowledge of the real nature of morality (that it is a means to discipline and cultivate the human animal).

The passage I have selected for this chapter comes from 'Of Old and New Law-Tables' in *Thus Spoke Zarathustra*. It is one of the longest discourses in the text, composed of thirty sections and placed towards the end of part three. In *Ecce Homo* Nietzsche refers to this particular discourse as a decisive chapter in the book. It affords valuable insight into how he conceived the *Übermensch*, the superman or overman. In this discourse we encounter Zarathustra in patient mode. He has plenty of time on his hands and he is waiting for the hour to come when he will descend once more to human beings. He is sitting and waiting surrounded by old shattered law-tables and new half-written ones. Section two of the discourse speaks, not for the first time in the book, of good and evil. Zarathustra states that the only one who knows what is good and evil is the one who creates: the one that 'creates a goal for mankind and gives the earth its meaning and its future: he it is who *creates* the quality of good and evil in things'. The old metaphysical conceits about the creation of good and evil need to be overturned. Professorial chairs, the great masters of virtue, saints, poets and world-redeemers – all need to be taken to task on this issue.

And yet how is Zarathustra to speak to humans of all this? It is a deadly serious business and the mockery of past teachings can be bought cheaply. Even the new teaching can be quickly ruined and subject to miscalculation and misinterpretation (as if creating a new good and evil was something easy). Zarathustra confesses that he is ashamed that he too must speak like a poet and in parables. His wise desire has been born on the mountains – at a distance from humans – and this wild wisdom has looked into the becoming of the world, seen a world unrestrained and abandoned and fleeing back into itself, a world where time appears as a blissful mockery of all moments, where necessity appears as freedom itself, and where one encounters one's old devil and arch-enemy, the spirit of gravity, the spirit who created 'compulsion, dogma . . . purpose and will and good and evil'. This is the spirit with whom Zarathustra is in constant battle. It is from Zarathustra's efforts to outwit the spirit of gravity that he gives birth to the word *Übermensch*.

At the centre of the book is a new teaching of redemption. This is mentioned in the section under discussion and refers back to one of the most important discourses, entitled 'Of Redemption'. In contrast to the English word 'redemption' which suggests the payment of a debt, the German word *Erlösung* is connected with solution (*Lösung*) and dissolution (*Auflösung*), and thus names a setting free. Zarathustra asks, what is the will's loneliest affliction? In other words, what is it that causes the will most sorrow and grief? The answer he comes up with is that it is the fact that the will feels itself unable to break time and time's desire: '"It was": that is what the will's teeth-gnashing and loneliest affliction is called' (the same imagery is used here as was used in *The Gay Science* 341 on the eternal return). Because it feels powerless against that which has been done, the will becomes an angry spectator of all things past. Moreover, because it cannot will backwards the will comes to resent time itself. Only the future, however, can make amends for what happens in time; indeed, only the future can teach us what it means to say of the past, 'thus I willed it!' We need to think the future 'here and now', as that which interrupts the monotonous and stable rhythms of the present. The task is not to effect reconciliation with time past, but to redeem it through a new creation and action. Only this kind of redemption of time can free the will from the spirit of revenge that cripples its relation to time, in particular to time's essential pastness (the law of time is that time passes as a perpetual perishing).[14] This explains why Zarathustra is so keen to teach the necessity of action: 'Where is beauty? Where I *have to will* with all my will; where I want to love and perish, that an image may not remain merely an image' ('Of Immaculate Perception'). To live life, and to learn how to love it, requires that we touch it.

This discourse contains other important offerings. Although there are diverse paths to the task of overcoming, only a buffoon thinks that the human can be jumped over (section 4).

The noble soul is a soul for whom love is a work and a task; it desires 'nothing *gratis*, least of all life'. For noble souls, life has given something of itself and they always consider what they can best give in return. If life gives a promise, then the noble soul is one that keeps that promise to life (5). A new practice of knowledge must come into existence where knowledge will be free of the bad conscience (7). Indeed, up to now there has only been the appearance of knowledge of good and evil, a profound ignorance and self-conceit masquerading as divine or transcendent knowledge (9). One's compassion is necessarily directed to the past when one appreciates the extent to which it is always handed over. A new nobility is needed in order to guard against two things, the rule of a great despot who could come to compel and constrain all that is past until it became his bridge; and the rule of one who comes from the mob and who remembers back to his grandfather and no further, for time stops for him at this point. The new nobility will oppose all mob-rule and all despotism, writing upon new law-tables the word 'Noble'. This nobility will be made up of many different kinds and types of noble beings (11). The land that these noble ones will love is not the land of fatherlands and fore-fatherlands, but the children's land conceived as 'the undiscovered land in the furthest sea' (12).

The new teaching will contest the despair taught by modern nihilistic spirits who have made the decision against life and now assume the role of preachers of death, cheaply announcing that all is in vain – why live when it means to thrash straw? Why live when it means to burn oneself and yet not become warm? – that the world is a filthy place, that wisdom makes one only weary and so on. It is from such a mould that certain modern souls seek to ennoble themselves: 'Such people sit down to dinner and bring nothing with them, not even a good appetite – and now they say slanderously: "All is vanity!"'

(13). These modern spirits do not understand that it is no vain art to know how to eat and drink well. They 'have learned badly and the best things not at all, they have learned everything too early and too fast: they have *eaten* badly' (16). Those who are afflicted by life in this way do not know that spirit is a stomach and that their spirit is a stomach that aches and counsels death.

The contracts we make in life should be inspired by the art and science of living well, extending even to the marriage-contract. Should we not experiment and try 'a term and a little marriage, to see if we are fit for the great marriage! It is a big thing always to be with another!' The badly paired are always the most vengeful people, making everyone else suffer for the fact they are no longer single. Those who love each other need to see to it that they stay in love, or declare their promise to have been a mistake (24). Zarathustra's desire for life and for the earth is such that he anticipates 'new peoples' arising with 'new springs' rushing down 'into new depths' (25). 'He who discovered the country of the "Human", also discovered the country of "Human Future". Now you shall be seafarers, brave, patient seafarers!' (28).

Although Nietzsche wishes to protect the human being from all metaphysical bird-catchers who seek to teach it that it is of a different origin and higher goal, it is clear that he remains concerned with what may still become of the human ('the as yet undetermined animal', he calls it in *Beyond Good and Evil* 62). Is the superman a misguided fantasy on Nietzsche's part? Would not a genuine overcoming of the abstractions of metaphysics and ideals of morality require renouncing something like the superman? Much depends on what we take Nietzsche to be naming with the term. In *Thus Spoke Zarathustra* the term is not bound up with fantastical metaphysical speculation but simply denotes the new human type that has digested the news of God's death, seeks to practise the gay science, and renounces the metaphysics of morality. It is in his late writings (1885–8) that Nietzsche's ideas on the future of the human become fantastical and pernicious.

Nietzsche was honest enough to admit to his readers that a 'Thou shalt!' still pronounces itself in his writings. We might suppose that this makes him a supreme moralist, which was Freud's assessment. However, Nietzsche's moralism has peculiar and paradoxical conditions of existence. It sets itself a unique aim: that of showing human beings what is involved in the tasks of purification and renunciation (*The Gay Science* 285 and 335). This entails learning to live without the concept of God and without the 'curse' of the ideal. For Nietzsche the concept of God has been the greatest objection to existence so far. God names an ultimate Being that serves as a first cause and that would allow us to conceive the world as a unity. The world can be redeemed (freed) only by denying this concept. God is to be rejected as a crude answer to an intellectual problem and a prohibition against thinking. In *The Gay Science* 285 Nietzsche outlines the task of renunciation facing modern human beings and what it demands of them. We moderns will never pray again and never again live in endless trust; we will not allow our thoughts to unharness themselves before any ultimate wisdom, goodness or power; we are resolved to live without an avenger and without a final corrector of the text of our lives; we are not able to find reason at work in what happens, and no love in what happens to us; we arm ourselves against any ultimate peace and will the eternal recurrence of war and peace. We are beings of renunciation, and all of this we have renounced. But where can we find the strength to live like this? Nietzsche tells of a lake that one day refused to let itself flow off and formed a dam; ever since it has risen higher and higher. He concludes: 'Perhaps this very renunciation will lend us the strength to bear renun-ciation; perhaps man will rise ever higher when he no longer *flows off* into a god.'

Nietzsche wants us to live without idealising and moralis-ing reality; and the challenge he presents to a new humanity, to which in *Thus Spoke Zarathustra* he assigns the task of remaining true to the earth, is whether it can still live and love life without this idealising and moralising. He was not sure that he himself had not been infected, deeply so, by the moralisation and idealisation he felt such contempt towards. It was this infection that Nietzsche suffered from most and that lends profundity and difficulty to his suffering.

9

NIHILISM AND THE WILL TO NOTHINGNESS

Except for the ascetic ideal: man, the *animal* man, had no meaning up to now. His existence on earth had no purpose; 'What is man for, actually?' – was a question without an answer; there was no *will* for man and earth; behind every great human destiny sounded the even louder refrain 'in vain!' *This* is what the ascetic ideal meant: something was *missing*, there was an immense *lacuna* around man, – he himself could think of no justification or explanation or affirmation, he *suffered* from the problem of what he meant. Other things made him suffer too, in the main he was a *sickly* animal: but suffering itself was *not* his problem, but the fact that there was no answer to the question he screamed, 'Suffering for *what*?' Man, the bravest animal and most prone to suffer, does *not* deny suffering as such: he *wills* it, he even seeks it out, provided he is shown a *meaning* for it, a *purpose* of suffering. The meaningless of suffering, *not* the suffering, was the curse which has so far blanketed mankind, – and *the ascetic ideal offered man a meaning*! Up to now it was the only meaning, but any meaning at all is better than no meaning at all; the ascetic ideal was, in every respect, the ultimate '*faute de mieux*' [for lack or want of anything better] *par excellence*. Within it, suffering was given an interpretation; the enormous emptiness seemed filled; the door was shut on all suicidal nihilism. The interpretation – without a doubt – brought new suffering with it, deeper, more internal, more poisonous suffering, suffering that gnawed away more intensely at life: it brought all suffering within the perspective of *guilt* . . . But in spite of all that – man was *saved*, he had a *meaning*, from now on he was no longer like a leaf in the breeze, the plaything of the absurd, of 'non-sense'; from now on he could *will* something, – no matter what, why and how he did it at first, the *will itself was saved*. It is absolutely impossible for us to conceal what was actually expressed by that whole willing, which was given its direction by the ascetic ideal: this hatred of the human, and even more of the animalistic, even more of the material, this horror of the senses, of reason itself, this fear of happiness and beauty, this longing to get away from appearance, transience, growth, death, wishing, longing itself – all that means, let us dare to grasp it, a *will to nothingness*, an aversion to life, a rebellion against the most fundamental prerequisites of life, but it is and remains a *will*! . . . And, to conclude by saying what I said at the beginning: man still prefers to *will nothingness*, than *not* will . . .

Extract from *On the Genealogy of Morality*, essay 3, aphorism 28

Although the problem of nihilism dominates Nietzsche's late thinking we do not find extensive treatments of it in his published writings. The most important sources are book five of *The Gay Science* and *On the Genealogy of Morality*, especially its third essay. In the unpublished writings from this period, however, we find a number of notebooks on nihilism. The most important of these is the one entitled 'European Nihilism', dated June 1887, and known as 'Lenzer Heide' (Spring Heath), which refers to the place in the Upper Engadine where Nietzsche composed it on the eve of writing *On the Genealogy of Morality* in July and August of that year. This notebook is close to the concerns of the third essay of *On the Genealogy of Morality* and in it is to be found, as we shall see, another working of eternal recurrence.[15]

This aphorism is the final one in *On the Genealogy of Morality*, forming the denouement to the book's third and last essay, which takes the form of an inquiry into ascetic ideals, ideals of denial and mortification of the will. Nietzsche couches this as an inquiry into their meaning or significance (*Bedeutung*). It is clear from this final aphorism of the book that his questioning of them is also a questioning of the sense and direction (*Sinn*) of the human will itself. Nietzsche clarifies the specific nature of his inquiry in section 23 of the essay. Here he speaks of the ascetic ideal as a generic term and says that the issue of what it signifies is to be approached in terms of an analysis of 'what lies behind, beneath and within it' and 'what it expresses in a provisional, indistinct way, laden with question marks and misunderstandings'. In short, the task is to bring this ideal to self-knowledge by uncovering what lies concealed beneath it. Nietzsche holds that this ideal possesses a power; moreover, this power has a monstrosity to it, it has produced a monstrosity of effects that have been 'calamitous'. He wants to know why it has occupied so much space in human existence and why there has been so little effective resistance to it. He also poses the question, where is the 'opposing will, in which an *opposing ideal* might express itself?'

In the course of the essay Nietzsche treats a veritable array of phenomena with regard to his guiding question, including art and artists (sections 2–6), philosophy and philosophers (7–12), religion and the priest (13–22), science (23–27), atheism and the idealism of knowledge in general (25–27). Nietzsche's startling claim is that all these practices are implicated in the ascetic ideal and have an investment in it. Some readers may be sceptical about the enormous range of phenomena he implicates in the development of the ascetic ideal. For Nietzsche, however, that this ideal has been so prevalent in history, and continues to be so, reveals something essential about the human will, a 'basic fact', chiefly, that a '*horror vacui*' engulfs it and shows that it needs an aim or goal – to the point that 'it prefers to will *nothingness* rather than *not* will'.

Nietzsche is conscious of the fact that with the formulation 'will to nothingness' he is deliberately subverting Schopenhauer for whom willing and nothingness are mutually exclusive conditions. Once we have recognised that incurable suffering and perpetual misery are the essential features of the phenomenon of the will to life and we see the world melt away with the abolition of this will, then we retain before us only empty nothingness. For Schopenhauer this can become our great consolation. Nietzsche's claim is that willing something is an inescapable fact of human existence and practices of self-denial, which involve the will turning against itself, remain expressions of willing (nothingness remains an aim or goal and names something be it God or Nirvana). Nietzsche is, in fact, developing an account of perversion and he is fascinated and disturbed by what he uncovers.

On one level the ascetic ideal appears to express a self-contradiction in as much as we seem to encounter with it life operating against life. Nietzsche argues, however, that viewed from physiological and psychological angles this amounts to nonsense. In section 13 of the third essay he suggests that on closer examination this self-contradiction turns out to be only apparent, it is 'a psychological misunderstanding of something, the real nature of which was far from being understood . . .' It is, he says, a term that is 'wedged into the old *gap* in human knowledge'. His argument is that the ascetic ideal has its source or origins in what he calls 'the protective and healing instincts of a degenerating life'. The ideal indicates a physiological exhaustion in the face of which 'the deepest instincts of life, which have remained intact, continually struggle with new methods and inventions'. The ascetic ideal is not what we might suppose; it is not, for example, a transcendence of the conditions of life (change, death, becoming) but a struggle with and against them. It amounts, in effect, to 'a trick for the *preservation* of life'. The disgust with life and nausea at existence that are at the heart of the ascetic ideal cannot transcend the conditions of life but only express them in specific ways. As Nietzsche points out, the ascetic priest's desire for being otherwise and for being in some other place than the earth contains an essential ardour and passion in which the '*power* of his wishing' is a fetter that continues to bind him to it. This binding is what makes him a tool that 'has to work to create more favourable circumstances for our being here and being man . . .' This negative human type belongs, ironically, to 'the really great conserving and yes-creating forces of life'.

How is the sickness of man possible? How is it to be explained? Nietzsche's answer refers us back to the opening of the second essay of the *Genealogy*: as a creature of time and memory, man has the potential to suffer greatly and deeply from himself. As the sick animal *par excellence* the human has 'dared more, innovated more, braved more, challenged fate more than all the rest of the animals taken together'. The human is an animal that freely experiments on itself and struggles for supreme control over animals, nature and gods. Man is the 'still-unconquered futurist' whose future 'digs mercilessly into the flesh of every present like a spur . . .' This courageous and rich animal is at the same time, on account of this courage and richness, also the most endangered and the one that suffers from an acute illness of life. Nietzsche refers to there being times in history when entire epidemics of being fed up with life have swept into existence and overtaken a people. But he notes that even this nausea at existence and fatigue in the face of it serve to propel the human forward in the direction of new creations and inventions, so that within the 'no' that it brings to life there is also a 'wealth of tender "yeses"': even in our self-destruction we invent a wound that compels us to live. For Nietzsche, then, sickness in man has to be understood as a normal state. The real drive of the human animal is not to attain the salvation of its soul but to experiment on itself. We are self-violators, 'nutcrackers of the soul', who question and are questionable. The critical question Nietzsche poses is this: can we be equal to the event of this questioning? If we are able to be more deserving of asking questions we may become more deserving of living.

What is the basis of Nietzsche's objection to the ascetic ideal? He takes it to task on account of its fundamental dishonesty: it invests in something supposedly higher and nobler when, in truth, it is simply the investment of the energies and powers of life that it refuses to acknowledge (it does not know the nature of its own desire). For example, if a philosopher pays homage to ascetic ideals, as Schopenhauer did, for Nietzsche, it is because he has the strongest and most personal interest possible invested in it, namely, the desire of the tortured person to escape from torture. Nietzsche says he objects to the medication offered by the ascetic priest because it is not the medication of a doctor. The priest combats only the discomfort of the sufferer, not the cause and actual state of being ill. Of course, this does not prevent Nietzsche from admiring how much the priest sees and finds within this perspective. The priest is a genius in consolation and Christianity has developed a 'large treasure-trove of the most ingenious means of consolation' (means and methods of refreshing, soothing, narcotising), undertaking dangerous and daring risks for this purpose, subtly identifying 'which emotions to stimulate in order to conquer the deep depression, the leaden fatigue and the black melancholy of the physiologically obstructed'. All the great religions represent a fight against a weariness and heaviness of life that has become epidemic. Nietzsche offers as a general formula for what is called religion this non-conscious physiological feeling of obstruction that finds its mistaken cause and cure on the psychological-moral level (for example, through the invention of paralogical concepts such as guilt and sin).

Nietzsche holds that the great danger of this human sickness, which is also bound up with an unavoidable fear of man, is that it will lead not to the promotion of higher and rarer types but to the opposite, to a levelling out and homogenisation in which social and political institutions will exist simply to contain man. The danger is that we will allow society to nurture a false sympathy over the human condition. It is not fear of man we should seek to overcome, since this can serve as a spur to new experiments and tasks, but rather nausea at and compassion for him, for this will produce only the '"last will" of man, his will to nothingness, nihilism'. Nietzsche is fully cognisant of the fact that a goal cannot be ascribed to human history; rather, a goal can only be put in it. If we have need of a goal it is because we have need of a will – 'which is the spine of us'.[16] Nietzsche seems to have felt this spine in his own philosophical being in a peculiarly acute manner.

As he identifies it, the problem is not the mere fact that we suffer from life, but that this suffering needs an explanation and justification. He notes that the human animal can even will its suffering so long as it can be given a meaning and a direction. The interpretation of suffering developed by the ascetic ideal has succeeded in shutting the door on a suicidal nihilism. It has added new dimensions and layers to suffering by making it deeper and more internal; creating a suffering that gnaws more intensely at life and bringing it within the perspective of guilt or moral debt. But this saving of the will has been won at the expense of the human future and led to the cultivation of a hatred of the conditions of human existence. It expresses a fundamental will to nothingness, a 'fear of happiness and beauty' and 'a longing to get away from appearance, transience, growth, death'.

The notebook of June 1887 on European Nihilism begins by noting that the 'Christian-moral hypothesis' offered humankind a number of advantages, such as endowing man with an absolute value in the midst of his cosmic smallness and the flux of becoming. It also served the advocates of God in giving the world the character of perfection, in which evil and suffering could be granted a meaning. Most importantly of all, it protected man from despising himself and from despairing of knowledge. In sum, Nietzsche says, it was the great anti-dote to theoretical and practical nihilism. Nihilism can no longer be avoided simply because this hypothesis has collapsed and lost all credibility. Nihilism, however, is to be treated as a pathological transitional stage: we move from one extreme position (nature and the world have a meaning and a purpose) to another extreme position (all is devoid of meaning and purpose). If nihilism comes to us now as an uncanny guest it is not because the unpleasant character of existence is any greater than before, but simply because we are now mistrust-ful of *any* meaning in existence and *everything* appears to us to be in vain. Nietzsche stresses that to persist with this 'in vain', without aim or purpose, is the thought that paralyses the most. It is at this point that he re-introduces the hypo-thesis of eternal recurrence as the most extreme form of nihilism. It is such because it posits existence as it is without meaning or goal and eternally recurring without any end into nothingness. He compares it to a European form of Buddhism and notes that the doctrine has scholarly presuppositions, as did the doctrines of Buddha. To be a modern nihilist is to be in a relatively well-off position on a spiritual and cultural level since it presupposes a degree of intellectual culture and thus relative prosperity.

On the level of pathology nihilism is a symptom of those who have come off badly in life and find themselves deprived of any consolation. For these unhealthy types, who can be found in all classes he says, the eternal recurrence will be experienced as a curse. These are types who say 'no' after existence has lost its meaning and who destroy only in order to be destroyed in return. Their lust for destruction thus has an absurd character to it. They gnash their teeth and fanatically pursue a will to destruction, '*extinguishing* everything which lacks aim and meaning'. This so-called active nihilism is, in fact, a reactive nihilism. Nietzsche envisages a crisis taking place in which different forces will come together and collide and there will be assigned 'common tasks to human beings with opposite ways of thinking', leading to the initiation of '*an order of rank among forces*'. He asks who in this struggle will prove to be the strongest and states that it is not a matter of numbers or of brute strength. The strongest will be the most moderate ones who do not need extreme articles of faith, but can concede a good deal of contingency and nonsense and even love it, and who can think of man with a moderation of his value without becoming small and weak in return. These are the ones who are rich in health, equal to the misfortunes of life and therefore less afraid of them, and who are sure of their power. Nietzsche concludes this notebook by asking what the spiritually mature human being would think of eternal recurrence. In other notebooks from this period he outlines eternal recurrence as a great cultivating thought that will provide a new principle of (artificial) selection and breeding by serving to strengthen the strong and paralyse the weak and disaffected.

Although Nietzsche is a severe critic of the ascetic ideal he cannot give up on the idea that the human will requires a meaning and direction. His preoccupation with this issue gives rise to serious problems in his late work. In *The Anti-Christ* (1888) he defines the 'good' in terms of everything that heightens the feeling of power (the will to power) and the 'bad' in terms of everything that proceeds from weakness; he proposes that 'the weak and ill-constituted shall perish: first principle of *our* philanthropy' (*The Anti-Christ* 2). These are not the words of an enlightened and mature philosopher but of an animal that continues to remain sick. Nietzsche defines the problem as one of deciding what 'ought' now to succeed mankind in the sequence of species and what type of human being 'ought' now to be bred as one that will be more worthy of life and certain of the future. This more valuable type, he says, has existed before but only as a lucky accident; it is now to be 'willed' and in opposition to 'the domestic animal, the herd animal, the sick animal – the Christian . . .' This 'higher type' is what he names 'the superman' (*The Anti-Christ* 3 and 4). Although there is nothing racialist in Nietzsche's conception of this programme of breeding and selection, it is without doubt the most disturbing aspect of his thinking. It is hard to deny that in the late writings Nietzsche's elevating 'ideals' of will to power, eternal recurrence and the superman – their elevating character is on display in *Thus Spoke Zarathustra* – degenerate into something fantastical and grotesque.

Whilst Nietzsche's analysis of the phenomenon of European nihilism is instructive, it is also deeply problematic. It remains too centred on a crisis of meaning and, as a result, it perpetuates the very thing it seeks to overcome, namely, metaphysics. As the most extreme form of nihilism eternal recurrence is offered as the solution to this crisis. But meaninglessness remains tethered to the problem of meaning, and affirming meaninglessness returning eternally is hardly a solution to it. The problem does not, in fact, need resolving but dissolving. Furthermore, the quasi-cosmological (metaphysical) configuration of eternal recurrence at work in the 1887 notebook does not serve well the ends of Nietzsche's own

thinking. It crushes all claims to absolute singularity by rela-
tivising our world in the midst of an infinity of recurring
worlds, and whilst it contradicts the Judeo-Christian idea of a
unique history governed by a divine dispensation that will
bring about the salvation of humankind, it does so at the
price of destroying all concrete polemics. Nietzsche's idea of
using the doctrine of eternal recurrence so as to forge a selection of the strong over the weak belongs to the realm of
vengeful fantasy.

10

BEHOLD THE MAN

Seeing that I must shortly approach mankind with the heaviest demand that has ever been made on it, it seems to me indispensable to say *who I am*. This ought really to be known already: for I have not neglected to 'bear witness' about myself. But the disparity between the greatness of my task and the *smallness* of my contemporaries has found expression in the fact that I have been neither heard nor even so much as seen. I live on my own credit, it is perhaps merely a prejudice that I am alive at all? . . . I need only to talk with any of the 'cultured people' who come to the Ober-Engadin in the summer to convince myself that I am *not* alive . . . Under these circumstances there exists a duty against which my habit, even more the pride of my instincts revolts, namely to say: *Listen to me! for I am thus and thus. Do not, above all, confound me with what I am not!*

I am, for example, absolutely not a bogey-man, not a moral-monster – I am even an antithetical nature to the species of man hitherto honoured as virtuous. Between ourselves, it seems to me that precisely this constitutes part of my pride. I am a disciple of the philosopher Dionysos, I prefer to be even a satyr rather than a saint. But you have only to read this writing. Perhaps I have succeeded in giving expression to this antithesis in a cheerful and affable way – perhaps this writing had no point at all other than to do this. The last thing *I* would promise would be to 'improve' mankind. I erect no new idols; let the old idols learn what it means to have legs of clay. *To overthrow idols* (my word for 'ideals') – that rather is my business. Reality has been deprived of its value, its meaning, its veracity to the same degree as an ideal world has been *fabricated* . . . The 'real world' and the 'apparent world' – in plain terms: the *fabricated* world and reality . . . The *lie* of the ideal has hitherto been the curse on reality, through it mankind itself has become mendacious and false down to its deepest instincts – to the point of worshipping the *inverse* values to those which alone could guarantee it prosperity, future, the exalted *right* to a future.

Extract from *Ecce Homo*, foreword sections 1 and 2

Two main features about Nietzsche's late writings need to be noted. The first is that they are written as a philosophy of the future and seek to herald this philosophy as an event. The second is that, in contrast to what he saw as the 'yea-saying' part of his task carried out in his previous writings from 1878 onwards, they belong to what he called the 'nay-saying' part, such as demanding a revaluation of values and heralding a great day of decision. From this point on, he says, all his writings are fish-hooks and are looking for fish; in other words, they are attempts to seduce (*amor* comes from *amus*, the Latin word for hook).

Nietzsche's planned magnum opus, to which he gave the working title 'Will to Power: Attempt at a Revaluation of All Values', never came to fruition. However, something of its nature can be found in the texts *Twilight of the Idols* (published in 1889) and *The Anti-Christ* (published in 1895 and regarded by Nietzsche as the first book of the revaluation of all values). With these works his campaign against morality, notably Christian morality, assumes an increasingly belligerent tone. In 1886 he composed a set of new prefaces to his back catalogue of published texts, which are among the finest pieces of philosophical self-reflection Nietzsche wrote. He admits to being something of a 'bird-catcher' himself, and to working against the unscientific tendency of a romantic pessimism that would inflate personal experience into universal judgement. Nietzsche is keen to counter this tendency in his own thinking.

Only towards the end of his sane life did Nietzsche's writings begin to attract the attention of European writers and intellectuals (for example, Hippolyte Taine and August Strindberg). Nietzsche himself regarded it as a comic fact that he was beginning to have a subterranean influence among a diverse array of radical parties and circles. He says that at the age of forty-three he feels as alone as when he was a child. He speaks of his solitude in terms of a condemned destiny, in which the unusual and difficult task that commands him to continue living also compels him to avoid people and to be free of all normal human bonds. Nietzsche thought that it should be neither necessary nor desirable to argue in his favour, and suggested instead that a more intelligent attitude towards him would be to adopt the pose one would in the presence of a foreign and alien plant – namely, one of curiosity and ironic resistance. In a letter written in December of 1887 to the Danish critic Georg Brandes, the first person ever to lecture on his work, Nietzsche responded favourably to his description of his thinking as an 'aristocratic radicalism'.

In 1888 Nietzsche spent what turned out to be his last summer in Sils-Maria. Earlier in the year he had written to his friend Franz Overbeck that the world should expect no more beautiful things from him just as one should not expect a suffering and starving animal to attack its prey with grace. He confesses to being devoid of a refreshing and healing human love and speaks of his absurd isolation which makes the residues of a connection with people something that only wounds him. In another letter from the early part of this year he speaks of himself as a sick animal and *la bête philosophe*. He is aware that the philosopher who embarks on a relentless struggle against everything that human beings have hitherto revered will be met with a hostile public reception, one that will condemn him to an icy isolation, with his books being judged in the language of pathology and psychiatry. He resolved to set time aside to tackle what he called the 'psychological problem' of the remarkable Danish thinker Søren Kierkegaard (1813–55). He never spells out what he means in referring to Kierkegaard in this way, and we can only be intrigued by it. In his last years of sanity Nietzsche developed a liking for the city of Turin. In it he found not a modern metropolis but, he wrote, a 'princely residence of the seventeenth century' possessing an aristocratic calm with no petty suburbs and a unity of commanding taste. He especially liked the beautiful cafés, the charming sidewalks, the organisation of trams and buses, and the fact that the streets were clean.

Nietzsche began work on *Ecce Homo* on his forty-fourth birthday, saying that the text was his way of testing what could be done with 'German ideas of freedom of speech'. He wanted to speak about himself and his writings with 'all possible psychological cunning and gay detachment'. The last thing he wanted, he confided, was to be treated as some kind of prophet and he hoped it would prevent readers from confusing him with what he was not. The title refers not only to Pontius Pilate's famous words about Christ, but also to those used by Napoleon when he greeted Goethe, '*Voilà un homme!*' Nietzsche interpreted this declaration as meaning, 'here is a man, when I expected a mere German' (*Beyond Good and Evil* 209). It is clear that Nietzsche, too, did not wish to be thought as a 'mere German'. He presents himself as a 'good European', as the 'last anti-political German', as Polish, as an admirer of French culture and so on; in short, anything but a mere German. At this time he also wrote to various people saying that his health had never been better. He drafted various letters, including one to Kaiser Wilhelm II and one to his sister in which he informs her that he is compelled to part with her for ever. Nietzsche had already sought to do so in an irrevocable manner several times before. The immense gulf that he felt separated them was, in large part, due to her anti-Semitism.

In December *Ecce Homo* was sent to the publishers and Nietzsche was observed by his landlady chanting and dancing naked in his room. On the morning of 3 January 1889 as he was taking a stroll through Turin's Piazza Carlo Alberto, he witnessed a carriage driver beating a horse. He threw his arms around the horse's neck and then collapsed to the ground, losing consciousness. In the course of the next few days he composed a series of infamous letters: he wrote to Gast announcing that the world had become transfigured; to Brandes, his champion in Copenhagen, that now he had discovered him the great difficulty was how to lose him; to Cosima Wagner, Wagner's widow, he wrote 'Ariadne, I love you'; to Overbeck that he was having all anti-Semites shot; and to Jacob Burckhardt, his former colleague at Basel, that he was all the names in history. Burckhardt showed the letter he had received to Overbeck, who then travelled to Turin and brought Nietzsche back to Basel. As Rüdiger Safranski, one of Nietzsche's biographers, notes, Nietzsche's philosophical history ends in January 1889. Then commences another history, that of his influence and resonance, which still continues today.

Although *Ecce Homo* turned out to be Nietzsche's last book, it was not intended to be. He had plans for new projects, but chose at that time to conduct a review of his writings to date and to instruct his future readers. The book is a cheerful one, with ironically titled chapters such as 'Why I am so wise',

'Why I write such good books' and 'Why I am destiny'. It is subtitled 'How One Becomes What One Is', a phrase taken from one of Pindar's Pythian odes from the fifth century BC, which says 'become the one you are' ('*genoi hoios essi*') (see also *The Gay Science* 270). However, in the foreword and other places in the book, he puts the emphasis on the issue of 'who' he is. He tells us that he is a disciple of Dionysos – who is to be understood as a philosopher (see *Beyond Good and Evil* 295) – and that he prefers to be a lustful man (a satyr) rather than a saint. Although he is an immoralist who philosophises beyond good and evil he is not, he says, a moral monster. His writings are not given over to the task of improving humanity and he erects no new idols (his word for 'ideals'). He has devoted himself to exposing the 'lie' of the ideal and he wants humanity to earn the 'exalted *right* to a future'. It could be suggested that in speaking of himself in this way Nietzsche is at war with himself, battling with the complex legacy his new teaching will bequeath to future readers: we have to renounce so many things, and yet we have to still believe in so many things; we have to give up on our ideals and yet we are to set ourselves new tasks and be severe on ourselves, indeed, we moderns have to be more severe on ourselves than any previous humanity.

Nietzsche's appeal to Dionysos reappears in his late writings. In the section entitled 'What I Owe to the Ancients' in *Twilight of the Idols* the Dionysian is presented as a faith in which 'the most profound instinct of life', the instinct for its future and eternity, is felt in a religious manner. In the Dionysian mysteries it is possible to locate 'the eternal return of life', in which the future is consecrated in the past and there is a triumphant affirmation of life over and above death and change. Nietzsche later noted that his first published book, *The Birth of Tragedy*, was silent about Christianity, and he holds this silence to be both a cautious and hostile affair. Only in his late work, in fact, does he position Dionysos against the figure on the cross as its complete and ultimate antithesis. *Ecce Homo* closes with the words: 'Have I been understood? *Dionysos against the Crucified*'. Nietzsche posits the difference between them as a difference in the meaning of their martyrdom. In the Christian case, which represents the Crucified as the innocent one, suffering counts as an objection to existence and is a path to a holy life; in the other case, 'being is deemed as *holy enough* to justify even a monstrous amount of suffering'. Whereas the god on the cross is a 'curse on life' and a signpost to seek redemption from it, the god Dionysus, cut to pieces, 'is a *promise* of life: it will be eternally reborn and return again from destruction' (T*he Will to Power* 1052). The concept of Dionysos is a concept of affirmation, but one that contains within it a fundamental negation: the Crucified and Christian morality. Each of the closing three sections of *Ecce Homo* carries the phrase 'Have I been understood?' Christianity is criticised for being the most malicious form of the 'will to the lie', for its 'anti-natural' morality, for inventing the soul in order to destroy the body, for sucking out life under the holy pretext of improving mankind ('morality as vampirism') and so on. Nietzsche construes himself as a destiny because he holds himself to have unmasked Christian morality in terms of an event that is without equal and a 'real catastrophe'.

Nietzsche tells us that what inspired him to write *Ecce Homo* was a desire to stop people from doing mischief with his work, and he would do this by telling his readers who he is. But how reliable a witness is Nietzsche? Certainly the portrait he gives of himself in *Ecce Homo* is a complex, multi-faceted and perplexing one. On the one hand, we are presented with the voice of destiny ('One day my name will be associated with the recollection of something frightful – of a crisis like no other before on earth'), a voice that foretells of great and terrifying things to come: 'there will be wars the like of which we have never yet seen on earth'. On the other hand, this voice of destiny is keen to give us recommendations on what we should eat and drink (avoid coffee since it makes one gloomy; tea is OK but only beneficial in the morning and so on). He advises us to practise a form of sagacity and self-defence that would enable us to react to people and situations as seldom as possible; to not read too many books, but only a few cherished ones (to read a book in the freshness of the morning is, he says, quite vicious); to avoid becoming like the scholar who does nothing but trundle books and eventually loses the ability to think for himself, able only to reply to a stimulus; to avoid reading rooms; to sit as little as possible and to not credit any thought that has not been born in the open air and while moving freely about; to be selfish about oneself if one is to have a chance of becoming what one is; to read Shakespeare as a great buffoon; and to understand Hamlet as the figure for whom it is not doubt but certainty that makes mad.

One commentator, Peter Sloterdijk, has indicted Nietzsche for indulging in *Ecce Homo* in an egocentric logic of self-justification. According to Sloterdijk, Nietzsche became a victim of what he himself had identified as the rancour of greatness (*Ecce Homo* '*Thus Spoke Zarathustra*' 5). Sloterdijk defines this in terms of an unhappy compulsion to see behind what one has been doing, entailing an incessant doubling of the self into what is spontaneous and what is remembered. In the case of Nietzsche the effort involved in wanting to reunite his greatness with his personal ego results in a suffocation of that greatness. For Sloterdijk, Nietzsche is engaging in an ego-centred self-assessment of non-egoistical creative processes. In spite of all his psychological wisdom, he constantly falls back into the posture of someone who wishes to be praised and valued by others, or to sing his own praises because of a failure on the part of his contemporaries to recognise his genius. Nietzsche thus continually exploits himself and capitalises on his own vitality and intellectual power: 'His new ideas were consistently devoured by the oldest structure of values, and the dead ego's compulsion toward self-assessment always prevailed at the expense of any vital efforts.'[17] Although this provides instructive insight into possible aspects of Nietzsche's authorship in *Ecce Homo*, it fails to capture its truly complicated character.

According to another reader, Alain Badiou, Nietzsche's event as a philosopher both fulfils and abolishes itself under the sign of madness. Of course, we know that Nietzsche went mad. For Badiou, however, the madness at issue is not simply that of a diseased mind but of philosophical hubris. Badiou argues that in Nietzsche's case this is the predicament of an 'anti-philosophy'. He justifies reading Nietzsche in these terms on account of what he detects as his sophistry and penchant for apocalyptic incantations. Badiou advances his interpretation of Nietzsche in the context of a critique of one that has prevailed in certain philosophical quarters to date. This is the interpretation of Nietzsche developed by the likes of Heidegger and Eugen Fink (1905–75), who both argued that Nietzsche's attempt to overcome Western metaphysics and morality through a revaluation of values remains fatefully burdened by its attempted inversion. For Badiou, however, the event of the new in Nietzsche is not an overcoming but an act and a founding break.

In *Ecce Homo* Nietzsche, in fact, vacillates between a discourse on the self-overcoming of morality through truthfulness and the proclamation of 'Dionysos versus the Crucified' as that which places a caesura into the world. On the same page in *Ecce Homo* that Nietzsche declares himself to be not a man but a piece of dynamite, he also says he might be a buffoon and describes the task of revaluation as one that requires humanity to dedicate itself to the act of a supreme coming-to-itself ('Why I am a destiny' 1). Nietzsche insists that he is not a founder of a new religion and that he wants no believers. We seem to be presented with a voice that is keen to have its authority questioned and ultimately overcome. However, it is difficult to deny that Nietzsche's final writings do, in fact, give voice to religious impulses and demagogic drives.

For Badiou, Nietzsche's final signature of 'Dionysus versus the Crucified' represents a founding or original politics (and to which philosophical thinking gets subordinated, even sacrificed). The problem with such a politics, Badiou says, is that it cannot tell the difference between what is real and what is prophetic. The event simply announces itself and, as such, it is trapped in the circle of its own fantastical declaration. Nietzsche tells us who he is and bears witness to this, but is there anything in reality that could vouchsafe for the truthfulness of Nietzsche's declaration and promulgation? He fails to grasp that politics has the event as its condition; instead the new event is grasped by him in thought alone and, as a result, it is unable to discriminate between its actual or effective reality and its announcement. Nietzsche, Badiou contends, was left with the fiction of his own creation of the new world and the old world. Badiou's anxiety over the fantastical elements of Nietzsche's thinking echoes concerns first expressed by Lou Salomé in her remarkably incisive appreciation of 1894. For Salomé, Nietzsche's entire experience amounted to a falling ill from thoughts and a getting well from thoughts. What constitutes Nietzsche's peculiarity, his tragedy and his grandeur, is that he made his own soul a model for the universe. In later life Salomé expressed her own preference for Freud over

Nietzsche: for the discoveries of sober rationalism over the desperate heroism of excessive questioning, which requires that we relinquish any aggressive wish to convert and the urge to convince and teach.

In conclusion, what can be said about Nietzsche's ideas and the tasks his thinking bequeaths? It is important that we distinguish between what is intellectually mature in his ideas, and genuinely challenging about them, and what belongs to the realm of philosophical fantasy.

Nietzsche makes an important contribution to a fundamental task of modernity that starts with Kant, namely, the project of developing and securing humankind's intellectual maturity. In his writings it is possible to observe the tremendous labours involved in this task and gain a deep sense of the problems that have to be negotiated. However, although he was a severe critic of Kant's lingering attachment to metaphysics, he himself could not renounce philosophy's pretension to legislate through the creation of new values and earning the right to proclaim 'thus it shall be!' (*Beyond Good and Evil* 211). Nietzsche's attempt to force a resolution of the problem of the human animal through a new breeding and selection is over-determined by metaphysical considerations and speculations (evident in the later configurations of the will to power, the superman and eternal recurrence). It is not only metaphysics we suffer from; and yet a great deal of his thinking is focused on this kind of suffering, to the point where his projected overcoming of metaphysics remains completely in the grip of its pathologies. His analysis of the complex character of the human animal and attempt to enrich our conception of the possibilities of human existence remain challenging aspects of his thinking. However, in his late work his noble 'ideals' for the transformation of man and the earth assume a grotesque form and display a cynical naivety. Although Nietzsche examines human pathologies in ways that are genuinely instructive, he pays scant attention to the social structures and economic realities which inform and shape them. His opposition to capitalism was strictly of the romantic kind and his final political thinking lacks a credible vision of social change and cultural transformation. In several key respects Nietzsche remained an idealist and a moralist. As a result his thinking can instruct us only so far.

NOTES

1 Eugen Fink, *Nietzsche's Philosophy* (1962), trans. Goetz Richter (London and New York, Continuum Press, 2003), p. 20.

2 In his *Critique of Pure Reason* (1781–7) Kant wrote, 'I entitle *transcendental* all knowledge which is occupied not so much with objects as with the mode of our knowledge of objects in so far as this mode of knowledge is to be possible *a priori*.'

3 Clement Rosset, *Joyful Cruelty: Toward a Philosophy of the Real*, trans. D. F. Bell (Oxford University Press, 1993), p. 49.

4 This citation is from a notebook of summer–autumn 1873 on the 'asceticism of truth', and can be found in F. Nietzsche, *Unpublished Writings from the period of* Unfashionable Observations, trans. Richard T. Gray (Stanford University Press, 1995), pp. 190ff. The essay 'On the Pathos of Truth' can be found in F. Nietzsche, *Philosophy and Truth: Selections from Nietzsche's Notebooks of the early 1870s*, trans. Daniel Breazeale (Humanities Press, 1979), pp. 61–9.

5 The German word Nietzsche uses for knowledge is *Erkenntnis*, denoting that which can be cognised and re-cognised, and so rendered familiar (*das Bekannte*). On the importance of the *unknown* (*das Unbekannte*) for Nietzsche see *The Gay Science* 374.

6 See the study by Paul-Laurent Assoun, *Freud and Nietzsche*, trans. Richard L. Collier, Jr (Continuum Press, 2000).

7 Contrast, for example, the early episode of the madeleine cake with the later episode of the death of the grandmother in Proust's novel *In Search of Lost Time*. See the sections entitled 'Overture' and 'Intermittences of the Heart'.

8 This conception of forgetting as an active process was in circulation in nineteenth-century psychology, for example in the work of the German philosopher and psychologist Johann Friedrich Herbart (1776–1841), with which Nietzsche was familiar.

9 See Kathleen Marie Higgins, *Comic Relief: Nietzsche's* Gay Science

(Oxford University Press, 2000), p. 85 (*The Gay Science* 339 is not, however, subjected to a reading by her).

10 Nietzsche uses two phrases for his doctrine: *ewige Wiederkehr*, translated as eternal return, and *ewige Wiederkunft*, translated as eternal recurrence (see *Twilight of the Idols* 'What I Owe the Ancients' 4 and 5). *Wiederkehr* is connected to *kehren* (to turn), and *Wiederkunft* to *kommen* (to come). The word *Wiederkunft* is used in German when speaking of the Second Coming of Christ (as Nietzsche is well aware, see *The Anti-Christ* 41).

11 See *Kritische Studienausgabe*, ed. Giorgio Colli and Mazzino Montinari (Berlin and New York, Deutscher Taschenbuch Verlag and Walter de Gruyter, 1967–77 and 1988), volume 9, 11 [163]. pp. 504–5.

12 A complete translation of this sketch can be found in K. Ansell Pearson and D. Large, *The Nietzsche Reader* (Basil Blackwell, 2005). It can be found in the original German in the *Kritische Studienausgabe*, volume 9, 11 [141], pp. 494–5.

13 Ibid., 11 [143], p. 496. Nietzsche explicitly treats eternal return as a teaching of repetition (*Wiederholung*) in some of his sketches of 1881. See, for example, *Kritische Studienausgabe* 9, 11 [165], p. 505.

14 This law has perturbed several great thinkers, including A. N. Whitehead, who wrote, in his major work *Process and Reality: An Essay in Cosmology* (1927): 'The ultimate evil in the temporal world is deeper than any specific evil. It lies in the fact that the past fades, that time is a "perpetual perishing"'.

15 This notebook has recently been published in English for the first time in its correct form. See *Nietzsche. Writings from the Late Notebooks*, ed. Rüdiger Bittner (Cambridge University Press, 2003), pp. 116–23.

16 See Nietzsche, *Writings from the Late Notebooks*, p. 124.

17 Peter Sloterdijk, *Thinker on Stage: Nietzsche's Materialism*, trans. Jamie Owen Daniel (University of Minnesota Press, 1989), pp. 44–5.

18 Gilles Deleuze noted, 'This text resonates mysteriously with Franz Kafka.' See his essay 'Nietzsche' in Deleuze, *Pure Immanence: Essays on a Life*, trans. Anne Boyman (New York, Zone Books, 2001), p. 101.

APPENDIX

This aphorism contains the first presentation of the death of God in Nietzsche's writings. Reading it is like encountering one of Franz Kafka's parables – eerily so.[18] Kafka was one amongst the numerous literary figures of the twentieth century to be an avid reader of Nietzsche and to be inspired by his ideas. Others include: Georges Bataille, Gottfried Benn, Albert Camus, André Gide, Hermann Hesse, D. H. Lawrence, André Malraux, Thomas Mann, Jean-Paul Sartre, George Bernard Shaw and W. B. Yeats.

The prisoners. – One morning the prisoners entered the workyard: the warder was missing. Some of them started working straightaway, as was their nature, others stood idle and looked around defiantly. Then one stepped forward and said loudly: 'Work as much as you like, or do nothing: it is all one. Your secret designs have come to light, the prison warder has been eavesdropping on you and in the next few days intends to pass a fearful judgement upon you. You know him, he is harsh and vindictive. But now pay heed: you have hitherto mistaken me: I am not what I seem but much more: I am the son of the prison warder and I mean everything to him. I can save you, I will save you: but, note well, only those of you who *believe* me that I am the son of the prison warder; the rest may enjoy the fruit of their unbelief.' – 'Well now', said one of the older prisoners after a brief silence, 'what can it matter to you if we believe you or do not believe you? If you really are his son and can do what you say, then put in a good word for all of us: it would be really good of you if you did so. But leave aside this talk of belief and unbelief!' – 'And', a younger man interposed, 'I *don't* believe him: it's only an idea he's got into his head. I bet that in a week's time we shall find ourselves here just like today, and that the prison warder knows *nothing*'. – 'And if he did know something he knows it no longer', said the last of the prisoners, who had only just come into the yard; 'the prison warder has just suddenly died'. – 'Holla!' cried several together; 'holla! Son! Son! What does the will say? Are we perhaps now *your* prisoners?' – 'I have told you', he whom they addressed responded quietly, 'I will set free everyone who believes in me, as surely as my father still lives'. – The prisoners did not laugh, but shrugged their shoulders and left him standing.

Extract from *The Wanderer and His Shadow*, aphorism 84

CHRONOLOGY

1844 Friedrich Wilhelm Nietzsche born in Röcken (Saxony) on 15 October, son of Karl Ludwig and Franziska Nietzsche. His father and both grandfathers are Protestant clergymen.

1846 Birth of sister Elisabeth.

1849 Birth of brother Joseph; death of father due to 'softening of the brain' following a fall.

1850 Death of brother; family moves to Naumburg.

1858–64 Attends renowned boarding-school Pforta, where he excels in classics.

1864 Enters Bonn University to study theology and classical philology.

1865 Follows his classics professor to Leipzig University, where he drops theology and continues with studies in classical philology. Discovers Schopenhauer's philosophy.

1867–8 Military service in Naumburg, until invalided out after a riding accident.

1868 Back in Leipzig, meets Richard Wagner for the first time and quickly becomes a devotee. Increasing disaffection with philology: plans to go to Paris to study chemistry.

1869 Appointed Extraordinary Professor of Classical Philology at Basel University. Awarded doctorate without examination; renounces Prussian citizenship and applies for Swiss citizenship without success (he lacks the necessary residential qualification and is stateless for the rest of his life). Begins a series of idyllic visits to the Wagners at Tribschen, on Lake Lucerne.

1870 Promoted to full professor and gives public lectures on 'The Greek Music-Drama'. Participates in Franco-Prussian War as volunteer medical orderly, but contracts dysentery and diphtheria at the front within a fortnight. Spends Christmas with Wagner.

1871 Works intensively on *The Birth of Tragedy*. Germany unified; founding of the Reich. Granted his first period of leave of absence from his University 'for the purpose of restoring his health'.

1872 Publishes *The Birth of Tragedy out of the Spirit of Music*. Lectures 'On the Future of our Educational Institutions'; attends laying of foundation stone for Bayreuth Festival Theatre.

1873 Publishes first *Untimely Meditation: David Strauss the Confessor and the Writer*.

1874 Publishes second and third *Untimely Meditations: On the Uses and Disadvantages of History for Life* and *Schopenhauer as Educator*. Relationship with Wagner begins to sour; makes his last private visit to him in August. They do not see each other for nearly two years.

1875 Meets musician Heinrich Köselitz (Peter Gast), who idolises him and becomes his disciple. Attends a spa in the Black Forest seeking a cure to his violent headaches and vomiting.

1876 Publishes fourth and last *Untimely Meditation: Richard Wagner in Bayreuth*. Attends first Bayreuth Festival but leaves early and subsequently breaks with Wagner. Further illness; granted full year's sick leave from the University.

1878 Publishes *Human, All Too Human: A Book for Free Spirits*, which confirms the break with Wagner.

1879 Publishes supplement to *Human, All Too Human, Assorted Opinions and Maxims*. Finally retires from teaching on a pension. First visits the Engadine, summering in St Moritz.

1880 Publishes *The Wanderer and His Shadow*. First stays in Venice and Genoa.

1881 Publishes *Daybreak: Thoughts on the Prejudices of Morality*. First stay in Sils-Maria. Sees Bizet's Carmen for the first time and adopts it as the model antithesis to Wagner.

1882 Publishes *The Gay Science*. Infatuation with Lou Andreas-Salomé, who spurns his marriage proposals.

1883 Publishes *Thus Spoke Zarathustra: A Book for Everyone and No One*, Parts I and II (separately). Death of Wagner. Spends the summer in Sils and the winter in Nice, his pattern for the next five years. Increasingly consumed by writing.

1884 Publishes *Thus Spoke Zarathustra*, Part III.

1885 *Thus Spoke Zarathustra*, Part IV printed but circulated to only a handful of friends.

1886 Publishes *Beyond Good and Evil: Prelude to a Philosophy of the Future*.

1887 Publishes *On the Genealogy of Morality: A Polemic*.

1888 Begins to receive public recognition: Georg Brandes lectures on his work in Copenhagen. Discovers Turin, where he writes *The Wagner Case: A Musician's Problem*. Completes in quick succession: *Twilight of the Idols, or How to Philosophise with a Hammer* (first published 1889), *The Anti-Christ: Curse on Christianity* (first published 1895), *Ecce Homo, or How One Becomes What One Is* (first published 1908), *Nietzsche contra Wagner: Documents of a Psychologist* (first published 1895), and *Dionysus Dithyrambs* (first published 1892).

1889 Suffers mental breakdown in Turin (3 January) and is eventually committed to an asylum in Jena. *Twilight of the Idols* published 24 January, the first of his new books to appear after his collapse.

1890 Discharged into the care of his mother in Naumburg.

1894 Elisabeth founds Nietzsche Archive in Naumburg (moving it to Weimar two years later).

1895 Publication of *The Anti-Christ* and *Nietzsche contra Wagner*. Elisabeth becomes the owner of Nietzsche's copyright.

1897 Mother dies; Elisabeth moves her brother to Weimar.

1900 Nietzsche dies in Weimar on 25 August.

SUGGESTIONS FOR FURTHER READING

For a long time the main publishers of Nietzsche were Penguin Classics and Random House (Vintage Books), but there are now editions of many of the texts from Cambridge University Press and Oxford University Press. A translation of the German edition of *Nietzsche's Complete Works* prepared by Giorgio Colli and Mazzino Montinari is being published slowly by Stanford University Press. The best available collection of his letters in translation is that edited by Christopher Middleton, *Selected Letters of Friedrich Nietzsche* (Hackett 1996).

The following texts will enrich the reader's appreciation of Nietzsche's philosophical concerns in his early period: *Philosophy and Truth: Nietzsche's Notebooks from the Early 1870s*, ed. and trans. Daniel Breazeale (Humanities Press, 1979), and *Philosophy in the Tragic Age of the Greeks* (1873, but not published by Nietzsche), trans. Marianne Cowan (Regnery 1998). The book that bears the title *The Will to Power* (trans. Walter Kaufmann and R. J. Hollingdale, Random House, 1967) should not be mistaken for Nietzsche's planned but never realised magnum opus; it is a collection of his notebooks from the period 1883–8 and was put together after his death by members of the Nietzsche-archive, including Peter Gast, and with Nietzsche's sister guiding its publication. Neither the order of contents nor the headings derive from Nietzsche. The book has served to give the erroneous impression that 'the will to power', conceived by Nietzsche as an attempt at a new explanation of all events, is the central doctrine of his mature thought; in the published writings, however, there are only two places where the theory of will to power is presented in methodological terms (*Beyond Good and Evil* 36 and *On the Genealogy of Morality* II, 12). A more reliable edition of the notebooks, restricting itself to the period 1885-8, has recently been published as *Nietzsche: Writings from the Late Notebooks*, ed. Rüdiger Bittner (Cambridge University Press 2003). For valuable insight into Nietzsche's notebooks of this period see the essay on the subject by Mazzino Montinari in his indispensable volume, *Reading Nietzsche* (1982), trans. Greg Whitlock (University of Illinois Press 2003).

A good starting-point for the reader new to Nietzsche are the books by his two post-war translators into English, R. J. Hollingdale, *Nietzsche: The Man and his Philosophy* (1964) (Cambridge University Press, 1999), and Walter Kaufmann, *Nietzsche: Philosopher, Psychologist, and Antichrist* (1950) (Princeton University Press, 1974, fourth edition). Two recent biographies available in English are Curtis Cate, *Friedrich Nietzsche* (Hutchinson, 2002) and R. Safranski, *Nietzsche: A Philosophical Biography* (Norton & Co., 2002). I also recommend Lesley Chamberlain, *Nietzsche in Turin: An Intimate Biography* (St Martin's Press, 1999). On Nietzsche and his sister see Heinz Frederick Peters, *Zarathustra's Sister: The Case of Elisabeth and Friedrich Nietzsche* (Markus Wiener Publications, 1985) and Carol Diethe, *Nietzsche's Sister and the Will to Power: A Biography of Elisabeth Förster-Nietzsche* (University of Illinois Press, 2003). For Salomé see Angela Livingstone, *Salomé: Her Life and Work* (Moyer Bell, NY, 1984). Salomé's book on Nietzsche was first published in 1894 and is still worth reading today, Lou Salomé, *Friedrich Nietzsche: The Man in His Works*, trans. Siegfried Mandel (Black Swan Books, 1988). For an excellent introduction to Nietzsche, including the development of his thought, see Eugen Fink, *Nietzsche's Philosophy* (1962), trans. Goetz Richter (Continuum Press, 2003). Fink's book also happens to be one of the finest works on Nietzsche ever written; of all the books on him I have read it is the one I admire and respect the most.

Important and seminal studies of Nietzsche include: Gilles Deleuze, *Nietzsche and Philosophy* (1962), trans. Hugh Tomlinson (Athlone Press, 1983); Michael Haar, *Nietzsche and Metaphysics* (1993), trans. Michael Gendre (State University of New York Press, 1996); Martin Heidegger, *Nietzsche* (1961), trans. David Farrell Krell et al. (Harper & Row, 1982; four volumes); Karl Jaspers, *Nietzsche: An Introduction to his Philosophical Activity*, trans. Charles F. Wallcraft and Frederick J. Schmitz (University of Arizona Press, 1965); Pierre Klossowski, *Nietzsche and the Vicious Circle* (1969), trans. Daniel W. Smith (Athlone Press, 1997); Karl Löwith, *Nietzsche's Philosophy of the Eternal Recurrence of the Same* (1978), trans. J. Harvey Lomax (University of California Press, 1997); Wolfgang Müller-Lauter, *Nietzsche. His Philosophy of Contradictions and the Contradictions of his Philosophy* (1971), trans. David J. Parent (University of Illinois Press, 1999); and Georg Simmel, *Schopenhauer and Nietzsche* (1907), trans.

Helmut Loiskandl et al. (University of Massachusetts Press, 1986).

On topics covered in the ten chapters of this guide, I recommend two books on *The Birth of Tragedy*: James I. Porter, *The Invention of Dionysus: An Essay on* The Birth of Tragedy (Stanford University Press, 2000); and Peter Sloterdijk, *Thinker on Stage: Nietzsche's Materialism*, trans. Jamie Owen Daniel (University of Minnesota Press, 1989). On Nietzsche's moral perfectionism see Stanley Cavell, *Conditions Handsome and Unhandsome: The Constitution of Emersonian Perfectionism* (University of Chicago Press, 1990); and Daniel W. Conway, *Nietzsche and the Political* (Routledge, 1997). For Habermas's critique of Nietzsche's influence see *The Philosophical Discourse of Modernity*, trans. Frederick Lawrence (MIT Press, 1987). For Camus I especially recommend *The Rebel*, trans. Anthony Bower (Penguin, 1971). For Foucault see his essay 'Nietzsche, Genealogy, and History', in M. Foucault, *Language, Counter-Memory, and Practice: Selected Essays and Interviews* (Cornell University Press, 1977), pp. 139–65; and his book *The Order of Things* (Routledge, 1992). On the death of God in Nietzsche see René Girard, 'The Founding Murder in the Philosophy of Nietzsche', in Paul Dumouchel, *Violence and Truth: On the Work of René Girard* (Athlone Press, 1988), pp. 227–47; and Martin Heidegger, 'The Word of Nietzsche: "God is Dead"', in Heidegger, *The Question Concerning Technology and Other Essays*, trans. William Lovitt (Harper & Row, 1977), pp. 53–115. One of the best accounts of Nietzsche on truth can be found in Alenka Zupančič, *The Shortest Shadow: Nietzsche's Philosophy of the Two* (MIT Press, 2003). See also Jean-Luc Nancy, '"Our Probity!" On Truth in the Moral Sense in Nietzsche', in Laurence A. Rickels (ed.), *Looking After Nietzsche* (State University of New York Press, 1990), pp. 67–89. Although my reading of *The Gay Science* 339 in chapter six differs from his in a number of significant respects, I have been greatly aided in my appreciation of it by William Beatty Warner's interpretation in his excellent book, *Chance and the Text of Experience: Freud, Nietzsche, and Shakespeare's* Hamlet (Cornell University Press, 1986). A particularly incisive reading of eternal return can be found in Howard Caygill, 'Affirmation and Eternal Return in the Free-Spirit Trilogy', in K. Ansell Pearson (ed.), *Nietzsche and Modern German Thought* (Routledge, 1991), pp. 216–40. For Cavell's imaginative utilisation of the thought see S. Cavell, *Pursuits of Happiness: The Hollywood Comedy of Remarriage* (Harvard University Press, 1981); for Deleuze's see G. Deleuze, *Difference and Repetition*, trans. Paul Patton (Athlone Press, 1994). See also Milan Kundera's novel *The Unbearable*

Lightness of Being, trans. Michael Henry Heim (Faber & Faber, 1984). On *Thus Spoke Zarathustra* see Heidegger, 'Who is Nietzsche's Zarathustra?', in David B. Allison (ed.), *The New Nietzsche* (MIT Press, 1985), pp. 64–80; *What is Called Thinking?*, trans. Fred D. Wieck and J. Glenn Gray (Harper & Row, 1968); Carl G. Jung, *Seminars on Nietzsche's 'Zarathustra'* (1934–39) (Princeton University Press, 1998) and Deleuze's *Nietzsche and Philosophy*. On the will to nothingness and the ascetic ideal see Christopher Janaway (ed.), *Willing and Nothingness: Schopenhauer as Nietzsche's Educator* (Clarendon Press, 1998), especially the editor's own essay; and Charles E. Scott, *The Question of Ethics: Nietzsche, Foucault, Heidegger* (Indiana University Press, 1990). On *Ecce Homo* and the late work see Alain Badiou, 'Who is Nietzsche?', trans. Alberto Toscano, in *Pli: The Warwick Journal of Philosophy*, 11 (2001), pp. 1–12; Gillian Rose, 'Nietzsche's Judaica', in Rose, *Judaism and Modernity* (Basil Blackwell, 1993), pp. 89–111; Sloterdijk above; Paul Valadier, 'Dionysus versus the Crucified', in David B. Allison, *The New Nietzsche*, pp. 247–62; and Sarah Kofman, 'Explosion 1: On Nietzsche's *Ecce Homo*', *Diacritics*, 24 (Winter 1994), pp. 51–70. For valuable insight into how 'maturity' gets played out in modern thought see David Owen, *Maturity and Modernity: Nietzsche, Weber, Foucault and the ambivalence of reason* (Routledge, 1994). For Nietzsche's influence on twentieth-century novelists a good place to start is Keith May, *Nietzsche and Modern Literature: Themes in Yeats, Rilke, Mann, and Lawrence* (Macmillan, 1988).

The Friedrich Nietzsche Society (Great Britain), founded in the early 1990s by a group of UK academics, holds an annual conference and publishes a journal twice a year. It has a useful website which also provides links to other websites devoted to Nietzsche: http://www.fns.org.uk.

The following websites can also be recommended:

www.geocities.com/thenietzschechannel
www.dartmouth.edu/~fnchron
www.hypernietzsche.org

INDEX

Aeschylus 11
Anti-Christ 49
anti-Semitism 109
Apollo 9–14
Apollonian, the 10, 11, 14
Archilochus 11
Aristotle 10, 14
art
  Nietzsche's gratitude to 68
  and reality 69, 70
Aryan 'master race' 83
ascetic ideal 47, 49, 94, 95, 97–100, 102
ascetic priest 98, 99
atheism 35–6, 74
Avesta 87

'bad', the 103
Badiou, Alain 113
Basel 109
  University of 8, 15, 20, 109
Bataille, Georges 119
Bayreuth 4
beauty 61–5, 67, 69, 70, 71, 89, 95, 100
Bedeutung 96
Benn, Gottfried 119
Brandes, Georg 107, 109
breeding 103
Buddha/Buddhism 101
Burckhardt, Jacob 109

Camus, Albert 10, 119
capitalism 116
Cavell, Stanley 8, 73

chance 66–7, 69, 70
cheerfulness 2, 5, 30, 33, 34, 36–9, 55, 57
chorus 11
Christ 108
Christianity 110
  Christian morality 4, 36, 106, 111
  'Christian-moral hypothesis' 101
  and consolation 99
compassion 59–60, 90, 100
conscience 81, 90
consciousness 53, 56, 57, 71
consolation 97, 99, 102
creation and destruction (*asha* and *druj*) 86
Crucified, the 111, 113
cultural renewal 4, 15

Darwin, Charles: *The Origin of Species* 22
death 12, 25, 26, 78, 90, 91
Deleuze, Gilles 73, 83
demon (*daimon*) 77–8, 79
desire 12
digestion 53, 54, 57, 84
Dionysian, the 9, 10, 11, 14, 16, 17, 20, 23, 110
Dionysus 9–13, 17, 29, 105, 110, 111, 113, 114
dissolution (*Auflösung*) 89

ecstasy 16
Egypticism 26, 28

Emerson, Ralph Waldo 8, 59
energy 12, 74
error(s) 47, 67, 76
eternal return/recurrence 5, 20, 29, 73–6, 78, 81, 86, 95, 101–4, 110, 115
Euripedes 12
evil 21, 86, 88, 90, 101
evolutionary theory 22

fate 67, 69–70
Fink, Eugen 113
forgetting 5, 52, 53, 55, 56–7, 59
Forster-Nietzsche, Elisabeth (Nietzsche's sister) 109
Foucault, Michel 2, 24
Franco-Prussian War 9
free spirit 4, 22, 33, 34, 49, 74
free will 21, 28
Freud, Sigmund 21, 53, 92, 114–15

Gast, Peter 20, 109
'gay science' 2, 32, 92
German culture 15
Gide, André 119
God 5, 28, 49, 97
    death of 30, 31, 34–5, 37, 39, 92, 119
Goethe, Johann Wolfgang von 8, 108
'good', the 102–3
good and evil 86, 88, 90
Gospels 31
Greek tragedy 9, 11, 12, 15, 69
Groundhog Day (film) 73
guilt 100

Habermas, Jürgen 16
happiness 95, 100
health 58, 85
heaviest weight 72, 74, 76, 80
Hegel, Georg Wilhelm Friedrich: Philosophy of Religion 34
Heidegger, Martin 83, 113
Heiterkeit 36
Hesse, Hermann 119
Hippocrates 3
Homer 9, 11, 77

humans
    capacity to make promises 53
    distinguished from animals 66
    drive of 98–9
    the sick animal 94, 98, 103, 107

ideals of denial 95
incorporation (Einverleibung) 46, 53, 54, 64, 71, 76, 77
individuation 12, 13, 14, 16–17

Kafka, Franz 119
Kant, Immanuel 10, 24, 28, 49, 115
    Critique of Judgement 8
Kaufmann, Walter 1–2, 31, 32, 39
Kierkegaard, Søren 108
knowledge 5, 6, 16, 21, 22, 24, 25, 27, 28, 32, 34, 37, 38, 39, 41, 42, 44, 45, 46, 48–51, 54, 61, 62, 68, 74, 77, 84, 90, 96, 101
Kundera, Milan: The Unbearable Lightness of Being 73

Lange, Friedrich: History of Materialism 8
language 26, 27
Lawrence, D. H. 119
life
    aversion to 95
    characteristics 12
    disgust with 97–8
    love of 38
    as a means to knowledge 39
    peaks of 64, 66
    saying 'yes' to 71
    as a seduction and a temptation 63
'Lord Chance' 66

Malraux, André 119
Mann, Thomas 119
meaninglessness 103
memory 5, 53, 55, 56–7
metaphysics 4, 28, 29, 103, 113, 115
moral world order 21, 36
morality 87, 92, 113
    Christian 4, 36, 106, 111

morality – *continued*
old 28, 29
sublime 29
music 11, 15

Napoleon Bonaparte 108
nature 8, 11, 12, 13, 17, 35, 53
Nazism 1, 83
Nietzsche, Friedrich Wilhelm
first philosophical essays 8
ill-health 9, 20
infamous letters 109
influences 7–8
'life is a woman' claim 61, 62–3
literary figures inspired by 119
madness 113
Professor of Classical Philology at Basel 8, 15, 20
relationship with Rée and Salomé 21–2, 85
in Turin 108, 109
and Wagner 9, 15
Nietzsche, Friedrich Wilhelm: works
The Anti-Christ 4, 40, 50, 102–3, 106
Beyond Good and Evil 4, 25, 28, 32, 43, 45, 50, 51, 73, 91, 108, 110, 115
The Birth of Tragedy Out of the Spirit of Music 4, 7–16, 20, 23, 37, 110
Daybreak 4, 27
Ecce Homo 4, 6, 20, 22, 32, 39, 58, 59, 85–6, 87, 105–6, 108–14
The Gay Science 4, 5, 30–40, 41–3, 45–6, 47, 50, 58, 59, 61, 64, 66, 68, 69, 70, 72–3, 75, 77, 79–81, 83, 89, 92, 95, 110
'Homer's Personality' (lecture) 9
Human, All Too Human 4, 18–19, 22–5, 36, 64
notebook on European Nihilism 101, 102, 103
On the Genealogy of Morality 4, 17, 23, 24, 38–9, 47–9, 52–3, 58, 94–5, 98
'On the Pathos of Truth' 43
Schopenhauer as Educator 37, 56
Thus Spoke Zarathustra 4, 5, 17, 22, 50, 66–7, 69, 73, 82–4, 85, 87, 91–2, 93, 103
Twilight of the Idols 4, 23, 26, 73, 106, 110
The Uses and Disadvantages of History for Life 54
The Wanderer and His Shadow 25, 119–20
The Will to Power 44, 111
Nietzscheanism 2
nihilism 2, 6, 9–10, 35, 39, 48, 90, 94, 95, 100, 101–2
Nirvana 97
nothingness 6, 96, 97

Oedipus 12
Overbeck, Franz 59, 107, 109

philology 2, 3, 8, 9
Pilate, Pontius 108
Pindar 11, 110
Plato 77
Platonism 26
positivists 28
principium individuationis 14
Prometheus 12
promises 53
psychology 21, 26
purification 92
purpose 21

reading well 2, 3, 6
reality
deprived of value, meaning and veracity 106
love of 68
ungodly 61, 64, 70
reason
categories of 44
providential 67
scientific 28
redemption (*Erlösung*) 13, 14, 88–9, 111
Rée, Paul 21, 85
On the Origin of Our Moral Sensations 21
Psychological Observations 21

renunciation 92, 93
resentment 57
Rilke, Rainer Maria 21
Ritschl, Friedrich 15

Sacrifice (film) 73
Safranski, Rüdiger 109
Salomé, Lou 21, 59, 85, 114–15
salvation 99, 104
Sartre, Jean-Paul 119
Schiller, Friedrich 11
Schopenhauer, Arthur 4, 10, 13, 14, 15,
    35–6, 39, 96–7, 99
  The World as Will and Representation 8, 15
science 16, 22, 23, 27, 28, 47, 48, 49,
    62
secularisation 74
selection 103
    principle 54–5
self-denial 97
self-knowledge 96
self-love 49, 50
Shakespeare, William 112
Shaw, George Bernard 119
Silenus 9–10
Sils-Maria, Upper Engadine region,
    Switzerland 20, 76, 107
sin 100
Sinn 96
Sloterdijk, Peter 16, 112–13
socialisation 74
socialism 74
Socrates 9, 73, 77–8
solution (Lösung) 89
Sophocles 11
soul, the 28, 36, 58, 61, 90, 99, 111
Spinoza, Baruch 20–1
  Ethics III 47
spirit of gravity 50
Strindberg, August 107
sublime, the 14–15, 28, 71
suffering 12, 59–60, 93, 94, 96, 98, 100,
    101, 111, 115

superman (Übermensch, overman) 2, 4, 5,
    28, 29, 82, 83–4, 87, 88, 91, 103, 115

Taine, Hippolyte 107
Tarkovsky, Andrei 73
theodicy 13
thermodynamics 73
time
    disappearance of 84
    forms of 65, 67
    the law of 89
tragedy 9, 11, 73
transfiguration 85
truth 5, 41–7, 49, 77, 87
Turin 108, 109

unconscious 53, 57
ungodly reality 61, 64, 70
unveiling 61, 62, 64, 65–6, 68, 71
Upper Engadine, Switzerland 20, 95, 105

vanity 90
veil, veiling 61, 63, 65, 67
'Vita femina' 5, 61, 66
Voltaire 19

Wagner, Cosima 9, 109
Wagner, Richard 4, 9, 16, 19–20, 109
Wagnerian opera 15
Wilhelm II, Kaiser 109
will, the 6, 8, 14, 15, 26, 35, 89, 95, 96
    mortification of 95
    will to life 97
    will to nothingness 95, 96, 100
    will to power 25, 27, 28, 46, 103
    will to truth 49
Williams, Bernard 2

Yeats, W. B. 119

Zarathustra 73, 82–9, 91
Zoroaster 86
Zoroastrian religion 75, 87